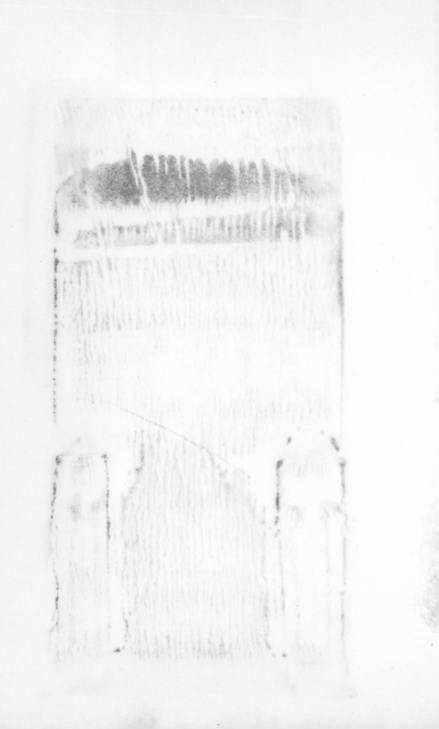

Living Personalities
of
The Old Testament

LIVING
PERSONALITIES
OF THE
OLD TESTAMENT

HAGEN STAACK

HARPER & ROW, PUBLISHERS
New York, Evanston, and London

To My Wife

Contents

Acknowledgments

This book (and the television series on which it is based) has been made possible by the help of a great many persons to whom I owe a debt of lasting gratitude. Here I can express appreciation only to a few. To the National Council of Churches and to the National Broadcasting Company I am grateful for the original opportunity to present the broadcast series. The editorial staff of Harper & Row gave valuable help in transforming material planned for television into book form. I owe special thanks to the following individuals who made indispensable contributions of time and skill: Mrs. Frank Deutsch, who helped prepare the manuscript; Miss Alice Parmelee, who provided invaluable editorial assistance; and my colleagues, Rev. Jesse Renninger and Dr. Rodney Ring, who generously gave expert advice and counsel.

H. S.

A Note to the Reader

This book seeks to introduce the general reader to some leading features of a part of the Old Testament story that spans many centuries. Much technical detail and scholarly apparatus has been omitted to achieve this goal within brief compass. The reader is encouraged to draw upon such other resources as those indicated on page 147 and in particular to accompany his reading by reference to the maps included in most Bibles or in the many Bible atlases available.

Preface

In the fall of 1962, the National Council of the Churches of Christ in the United States of America was given the opportunity to present thirteen half-hour programs over nationwide television on Sundays. After auditions, conferences, and screen tests, the author was commissioned by the Frontiers of Faith Committee to write the telescript and to deliver the messages before the NBC-TV cameras.

The instructions were that the subjects for the thirteen shows were to be taken from the Bible, but no other definite direction was given. The February, March, and April 1963 programs were to be the first attempt to present biblical topics to the television screen on a quarter-year basis. Teaching the Bible through television had been successfully attempted earlier, though for shorter time periods or with limited outreach. These programs had aroused enough interest to encourage the National Council of Churches to undertake thirteen half-hour programs of Bible studies for a wider audience.

That first series, on the opening chapters of Genesis, resulted in more than 15,000 letters, postcards, etc., being written to the National Council of Churches, to the network, and to the author. They came from people of all walks of life, of all age groups, and from all religious backgrounds. The favorable response caused the Frontiers of Faith Committee to commission a second series for February, March, and April 1964, again on material from the Hebrew Bible, the Old Testament.

This book, "Living Personalities of the Old Testament," was planned and prepared in conjunction with the television series of the same name.

The television medium imposes certain definite possibilities and impossibilities; imposes its own techniques on the choice of material and on its presentation; and because of this, imposes its own principles of selection and treatment on the writer and on the teacher in front of the camera. The half-hour programs form the rather limited framework, much too limited for the period of history to be covered. The topics, or persons, selected had to be fitted into this narrow frame. The selections had to exclude the great prophets except incidentally, in order to make possible a later series based on the prophets alone. Therefore, the varied history of the divided kingdom of the Hebrews had to be largely passed over, because it forms the background for the work of the prophets.

The decision was made to show some of the many "types" of people used by God in His historical dealings with a people He had chosen to become His Israel, with a special calling and mission in history. The history of the Hebrews is here seen through spotlighted individuals: in the spiritual leader Moses and in the folk hero of questionable character, Samson; in kings and in a foreigner from Moab; in the battle hero Joshua and in the impassioned reformer Josiah; and in the teacher Ezra, who laid the foundations of Judaism.

As Moses brought his people out of Egypt into the Promised Land, so Ezra helped bring the returnees from Babylon home to Judah and Jerusalem. This alone would constitute a fascinating theme: that Israel's history is a continuous return to a God-given home where the people are never really at home, for their role brings disturbing uncertainty rather than the life of un-disturbed peace reserved for the future Messianic Age.

The personalities chosen for the twelve chapters are the same as those for the television shows. These are arbitrary choices because under the label of Israel's history there is so much more than twelve television shows could contain. But the "types" brought together in these chapters, and correspondingly in the programs, illustrate a number of recurrent themes:

(1) God accomplishes his plan for Israel in spite of the people, not because of them. This plan is realized through a continuous adaptation of God's grace to the frailty of man.

(2) God uses all kinds of people. The Bible knows how differ-ent we are from one another, and that no two people are alike. History and revelation, law and life, would be much easier if human beings were more uniform. The Scripture portrays the human qualities of individuals and types.

(3) There are no "saints" in the Hebrew Bible. Even the great-est fail, and fail in important situations, so that Moses, for instance, was not allowed to enter the Promised Land, and could see it only from a distance. And the founding father of Judaism, Ezra, was in part a cruelly narrow and fanatical person, without much sign of love.

(4) God's historical revelation takes place within human his-tory, and therefore within the lives of real people who lived in concrete human relationships and in definite historic periods. The God of Israel is not abstract, a kind of absolute, but is involved in the processes of a creation He has made. He is the same One, from eternity to eternity, yet He created man within time, and man is a being who failed and who is loved by his Creator in spite of failure.

It has become a prevalent view among Christians to see the Old Testament as the Book of the Law, and to declare the New Testament the proclamation of God's grace. This makes the

Old Testament no more than a long training session under the impossibly demanding law of God.

I do not share this view, but think rather of the Old Testament as the book which proves that even before the coming of the Christ, man and the world were sustained only by the grace of God. The entire history of Israel, from Moses to Ezra, is the story of its sustenance by the Creator of heaven and earth—the God of Abraham, Isaac, and Jacob—in spite of its people. If full judgment under the law had ever been applied, utter destruction would have resulted.

The history of the Hebrews is, therefore, unlike any other history, and so the record of this history is unlike any other. The reader of the books of Scripture cannot be satisfied solely with reviewing historical facts, dates, and events. Nor can he stop with critical examination of the biblical texts, in order to reconstruct the highly complex process by which they came into their present, final form. Neither will it be enough to match the findings of archaeology with the biblical record, to deliver proof for the reliability of the Scripture as a historical document. We will have to use all the insights gained by historical research, literary criticism, archaeology, and other auxiliary sciences, but we do not want to stop there. The all-important work about, and with, and in the Bible is to discover that structure by which Israel's faith has built, out of the many events and persons, sources and repeated reinterpretations, its "history of the people of the covenant."

The Gospel according to St. Luke tells the story of the disciples on the road to Emmaus. They are joined by Jesus Christ, whom they do not recognize. As He comments on their sadness, they ask Him whether He is the only stranger in Jerusalem who does not know what happened to Jesus from Nazareth. The way they phrase their question reveals how little they understood their master; especially, how little they knew of the Scriptures. Jesus

Christ opens their eyes and "beginning with Moses and all the prophets, he interpreted to them in all the scriptures the things concerning himself" (Luke 24:27).

The part of the Bible we call the Old Testament was the Bible of Jesus Christ. He saw this Scripture as a witness to Himself, and for Himself. Certain prophetic passages have been interpreted too often and in too easy a fashion as pointing immediately and directly to Jesus Christ—as if the Old Testament were a kind of puzzle for which you need a key, and with the key, provided by the New Testament, everything falls into place. God's revelation is not a gradual evolution of man's religious consciousness, as man discovered himself more and more, progressing to higher levels, and thus shaping a better and higher image of God. The Scripture is not that man-centered. It is God who is in the center of the Old Testament and the New. He reveals Himself to man in such a fashion, always and everywhere, that man can grasp what is needed for the moment. Where man is too weak, He gives in; He bears patiently, and obviously permits actions that become unpermitted later on. It is not God who changes; but He has changed the amount of knowledge He knows man can absorb. We believe that Jesus Christ is the measure, with whom the level is reached that surmounts many levels of the Old Testament.

But the same One God speaks in the Hebrew Bible as in the New Testament, and this same One God is the father of our Lord Jesus Christ. This means that the New Testament cannot exist without the Old. For the early church, the Old Testament *was* the Scripture. The church existed for some time without a New Testament, as we know it, and yet was the true church of Jesus Christ. The comparative terms of Old and New Israel, old and new Adam, the Passover as understood and celebrated by the Jews and the Passover Lamb Jesus Christ—how can we know what is meant by one if we do not know the other? As the Old Testament law deals in an account of God's grace and is sustained only by grace, so in the New Testament the love of God in Jesus Christ is never without the law.

One of the amazing, and comforting, discoveries in serious Bible study is the fact that practically all major events and facts are reported by two, three, or even more sources, sometimes showing quite differing views. Traditions of very diversified backgrounds have gone into the making of our present Old Testament text. This means, in the final analysis, that the Old Testament cannot be used as a collection of prescriptions on how to conduct one's life. There are the Ten Commandments—but even there, varied interpretation and understanding are possible. Practically all the rest of Scripture forces us to make up our own minds in selection and study.

The Scripture is historic in two ways. It tells what takes place in history, and at the same time it is reported and interpreted by men within their historical limitations. We are bound, today, to our own history, our own place in time and in space. From the Scripture we learn, through fine examples, the exhortations, the warnings, the great images, but we are not relieved of the duty to conscientiously make up our own minds, make our own decisions, be responsible for our own sins. This is what St. Paul meant when he wrote: "Now these things happened to them [the children of Israel] as a warning, but they were written down for our instruction" (I Cor. 10:11).

Muhlenberg College　　　　　　　　　　　　　　H. S.
Allentown, Pa.

I

MOSES

THE LEARNER

HIS BIRTH

Moses, the great leader of the Hebrew Exodus from Egypt, was born into an apparently hopeless situation. When his mother thought of her baby's future, she must have felt certain that he would never grow safely into manhood. From his birth, Moses, like all other boy babies of his people, was doomed by an edict of the Pharaoh to an early death.

Even if her baby were to live, she could see only an intolerable existence for him. His parents were members of those Hebrew tribes that had become an enslaved people in Egypt working under taskmasters' whips. Groaning under their burdens, the descendants of Jacob longed for escape from bondage. Escape, however, was a fantastic dream. Only endurance was possible as they struggled to fulfill their quota of hard labor from one miserable day to another, unaware that their deliverer was at hand, that God had a plan for His Chosen People.

Though Moses' mother despaired for her son, she did for him what she could. With all the cunning at her command she concealed her baby from the authorities for three months, all the while dreading that his hiding place would be found.

"Now a man from the house of Levi went and took to wife

1

a daughter of Levi. The woman conceived and bore a son; and when she saw that he was a goodly child, she hid him three months" (Exod. 2:1-2). The factual biblical account implies much more than it states.

What would happen when she could no longer hide the baby? When a new crisis developed, perhaps she would find a way to meet it, as her ancestors had been doing for generations. Meanwhile, all her strength and resourcefulness were needed in the daily struggle for life.

AN ENSLAVED PEOPLE

Centuries before, when the rains failed and grass shriveled and died in their homeland pastures, Moses' ancestors, the family of Jacob, had entered the fertile valley of the Nile, for news had reached them that there was grain in Egypt. In return for permission to graze their flocks in the rich fields of the delta, they had given their services to Egypt. At the time, it was a mutually satisfactory arrangement. Scholars believe these famine-driven tribes may have belonged to an aggressive people called 'Apiru. These roaming Semites are mentioned in nineteenth- and eighteenth-century B.C. documents and in the famous Tell el 'Amarna letters.

As ancient records show, Egyptian border patrols often permitted destitute peoples of the East to cross the frontier. To give them food in return for their labor was probably not as altruistic as one might think.

Egypt is situated at the western base of the Fertile Crescent, that immense semicircle of arable land hemmed in between mountains, sea, and desert. At one end of this crescent, Egypt links Asia with Africa. One of the oldest highways known to man, the well-traveled Road of the Sea, ran along the Egyptian coast and, after crossing the eastern frontier, northward to the lands of the Fertile Crescent. Merchants in endless caravan trains as well as warriors of many countries used this road. Thus on her northeastern frontier Egypt was open to the world. There she confronted energetic, wandering, often hungry peoples pressing toward the green and inviting Nile valley.

This border frequently changed with the fortunes of war. When Egypt was strong her armies established outposts far to the north. When she was weak, peoples bent on conquest penetrated deep into the Nile valley, as in the case of the Hyksos. These were a powerful Semitic people from the north who overran Egypt, seized the throne, and dominated the country from the 15th to the 17th Dynasties. It was, therefore, both politically and economically wise for Egypt to offer to those driven southward in times of drought the needed food—at a price.

The Hebrew tribes of Jacob may have reached Egypt soon after the shepherd kings of the Hyksos established their rule over the country. During the period of Hyksos domination, the Hebrews were apparently well treated. Their situation changed, however, about 1550 B.C. when the native Egyptian forces expelled the Hyksos and instituted the brilliant 18th Dynasty. The statement, "Now there arose a new king over Egypt, who did not know Joseph" (Exod. 1:8), may refer to this Egyptian revolution.

The change of rule brought a new policy of harshness toward foreign groups such as the Hebrews. The descendants of Jacob were treated more and more severely, so that by 1290 B.C., when Ramses II came to the throne, their situation had become nearly intolerable. This Pharaoh was a builder. With forced labor he constructed new cities in the delta. He rebuilt the old capital, renaming it "House of Ramses." Egyptian documents state that he used 'Apiru labor for his huge projects. Exodus records that the Egyptians "set taskmasters over them [the people of Israel] to afflict them with heavy burdens; and they built for Pharaoh store-cities, Pithom and Raamses" (1:11).

Throughout the centuries of their enslavement in Egypt, the Hebrews apparently maintained their tribal relationships. They lived apart from the Egyptians in their own area of the land of Goshen in the Nile delta. And despite their oppression, their numbers grew.

THE PHARAOH'S EDICT

This large and vigorous slave population, however, posed a threat to Egyptian sovereignty. "Behold, the people of Israel are too many and too mighty for us" (Exod. 1:9), cried the new Pharaoh in words that still convey his dismay and foreboding. Though he "made the people of Israel serve with rigor and made their lives bitter with hard service, in mortar and brick, and in all kinds of work in the field" (Exod. 1:13-14), the more he oppressed them, the more they multiplied.

Fearing a rebellion on the part of his overburdened slaves, the Pharaoh took drastic action. He summoned the two Hebrew midwives, Shiphrah and Puah, and commanded them, "When you serve as midwife to the Hebrew women, and see them upon the birthstool, if it is a son, you shall kill him; but if it is a daughter, she shall live" (Exod. 1:16).

Into this desperate situation Moses was born. Though, as we have seen, the midwife did not kill the infant, and his mother succeeded in hiding him for three months, the time approached when concealment became impossible.

THE BABY IN A BASKET

The basket was his mother's idea. From flexible reeds gathered at the river's bank, she wove a container large enough to hold a baby. After making it water-tight by caulking it with pitch, she placed her son in his boatlike cradle and set him adrift among the rushes growing at the water's edge.

Surely everyone knows the story of how an Egyptian princess, bathing with her maids in the river, discovered the strange basket. At sight of the crying baby inside, her heart melted with pity. Though she knew at once he was a Hebrew child, she rescued him from the water and adopted him as her own son.

It was natural for her to choose as his nurse a slave woman. According to tradition this nurse was Moses' own mother, hastily summoned to the scene by her young daughter, who had all the while been watching to see what would happen to the helpless child. To Moses' mother the princess said, "Take this child away, and nurse him for me, and I will give you your wages" (Exod. 2:9).

The scheme succeeded beyond the mother's wildest dreams. During his formative years, her son would learn from her the traditions of the Hebrew tribes from which he sprang, but, as the princess' adopted son, he was entitled to an Egyptian education and access to the royal household. Only members of royalty or the higher priesthood could approach the Pharaoh, for, believed to be of divine parentage, he represented in his person the presence of the other world in this world. But Moses, by virtue of his adoption, could freely appear before the exalted ruler of Egypt and gain a hearing. A brilliant future in the Egyptian court now lay open to the once-doomed Hebrew baby.

Similar tales of rescue from untimely death were told about other great men of antiquity. This story, however, dramatizes two important factors in Moses' early life: his Hebrew origin and his Egyptian upbringing. Even his name suggests his twofold background. Exodus 2:10 states that his foster-mother "named him Moses, for she said, 'Because I drew him out of the water.' " This is based on an interpretation of the Hebrew word *Mosheh*. Scholars also point to the fact that the name of Ramses (Rameses), believed to be the Pharaoh of the Exodus, contains the same Egyptian syllable that appears in Moses' name, and in other pharaonic names such as Thutmose and Ahmose.

MURDER OF AN EGYPTIAN

While still comparatively young, Moses was given a responsible position to which his exalted rank entitled him. The Scriptures picture him supervising his own tribesmen as they labored for his grandfather by adoption, the Pharaoh. Overseeing slaves who worked under inhuman conditions was not to Moses' liking, for he was a sensitive person, as his story shows.

One day "he saw an Egyptian beating a Hebrew, one of his people. He looked this way and that, and seeing no one he killed the Egyptian and hid him in the sand" (Exod. 2:11-12). One can feel with Moses the sudden flare-up of hot indignation, the blinding temper that made him commit his rash act. Then came fear of the consequences and feverish efforts to erase all traces of his deed.

What good could it do to murder one taskmaster found beating a slave, when the whole Egyptian economy was based on slavery? But Moses acted out of sudden emotion, as he was to do again in his later years.

The next day he tried to intervene in a quarrel between two of his fellow tribesmen, but one of them asked, "Who made you a prince and a judge over us? Do you mean to kill me as you killed the Egyptian?" (Exod. 2:14).

Moses trembled at the question. His crime had been observed after all. What could he do? Fearing certain death in Egypt he decided to flee.

PASTORAL INTERLUDE IN MIDIAN

Moses went into the desert, where he encountered dangers almost as great as those he fled from. He experienced hunger and thirst, extremes of heat and cold, peril of wild beasts, and fear of enemies. There was no one to befriend him until he eventually reached the rugged country of Midian. There, as he rested beside a well, he watched seven young women laboriously drawing water to fill the troughs for their father's sheep. Suddenly a rough band of shepherds chased the girls away so that they could water their own flocks at the filled troughs. Outraged at this injustice, Moses drove off the shepherds and helped to refill the troughs. When the sheep had drunk, he escorted the girls to their home.

Their father was the priest Reuel. In some chapters of Exodus he is called Jethro—an indication of different sources in the text as we now have it. Moses and Reuel formed a close relationship ~d by mutual respect. The priest of Midian gave one of his daughters, Zipporan, to Moses as his wife, and in time a son was born to them.

Moses kept his father-in-law's flocks. This duty required a strong man able to defend himself and the creatures in his care against marauders and wild animals that preyed upon sheep. He learned how to live in an arid, uninhabited region with only his herd around him. The practical lessons he gained at this time were to stand him in good stead later on. Every moment he had to be alert to danger. His duties, however, left him many solitary hours to think. Alone in the wilderness, Moses' spirit was trained and tempered.

During this pastoral interlude, his life was tranquil though somewhat at a standstill. Moses himself was happy. Why should he remember his own people still groaning under their bondage in far-off Egypt? Why endanger his own safety, his own peace of mind for his fellow tribesmen?

Meanwhile, in Egypt, the Pharaoh put more pressure on the Hebrews and they "cried out for help, and their cry under bondage came up to God" (Exod. 3:23).

THE BURNING BUSH

Many of the great religions of the world had their beginnings in the desert. There, surrounded by a vast, awesome landscape, a man can be alone with his God. The desert either breaks a man with its monotony, hardship, and solitude or forces him to build a strong inner citadel of values and of faith. In the desert a man learns to listen to his God.

One day while tending Jethro's flocks, Moses led the animals "to the west side of the wilderness, and came to Horeb, the mountain of God. And the angel of the Lord appeared to him in a flame of fire out of the midst of a bush; and he looked, and lo, the bush was burning, yet it was not consumed" (Exod. 3:1-2).

Fire as a sign of the Divine Presence appears frequently in the Scriptures. The flames of the Holy Spirit at Pentecost were another manifestation of the divine fire. This same "fire" led Israel out of Egypt and through her years of trial in the desert.

As Moses watched in amazement a bush which flamed but was not consumed, he heard a voice calling his name. Scarcely knowing what he did, he replied, "Here am I." He was commanded to remove his shoes because the place on which he stood was holy ground. Then God spoke to Moses.

First God identified himself. The Scriptures say that "the angel of the Lord appeared in a flame of fire" (Exod. 3:2). Thus even Moses himself was not permitted to see God. Even in this divine fire, visible to human eyes, God was still truly God, too immense and exalted for man with his small and limited vision to see fully. God revealed His name to Moses: "I am who I am . . . The Lord [Yahweh], the God of your fathers, the God of Abraham, the God of Isaac, and the God of Jacob . . . this is my name for ever" (Exod. 3:14-15).

Though "I am who I am," the holy name, sounds like an abstract idea, the God revealed to Moses is concrete and the living core of history. Moses was shown that Israel's history is God's direct and immediate work. Israel had to discover that God is the One who really exists. Everything else exists only because of Him. Despite His transcendence, God is very much involved in the affairs of men: the Lord is in the midst of His people. He is the Eternal who continuously makes himself part of the temporal.

While he stood beside the burning bush, Moses received the promise of a new land of freedom, "a good and broad land, a land flowing with milk and honey" (Exod. 3:8), the land once promised to Abraham in his covenant with God. The coming Exodus under Moses was the continuation of the covenant relation with God which began when Abraham left his home to go where the Lord directed him. The covenant idea, like a scarlet thread, constantly reappears in the fabric of the patriarchs' stories as well as in those of Moses and the men and women who succeeded him. All these men and events were part of a divinely directed history, designed to bring to Israel, and to all men, knowledge of God and freedom under His law. Has any greater hope or promise been given to men?

The third insight Moses gained at the holy mountain concerned his own part in coming events. He learned that he was chosen to free his people from bondage and lead them to the Promised Land. Moses knew the Pharaoh too well to believe the task of liberation would be easy. What sign could impress the haughty ruler of Egypt to such an extent that he would modify his relentless policy toward his Hebrew slaves? Moses saw a long and severe struggle looming ahead.

Alone in the silent wilderness Moses asked himself how he could ever do what God required of him. The pattern of his life to this point, however, shows that he was better prepared to lead his people out of bondage than he realized. Bitter struggles awaited him, but the Scriptures do not picture peaceful solutions when men challenge the pharaohs of this world.

By the time of Moses' return to Egypt he had advanced a long way in his apprenticeship. From his own mother he had learned some of his Hebrew traditions and from his foster mother, an insight into Egyptian habits of thought. Though he had thrown away a brilliant future in Egypt by his crime and flight, he had already tested his ability to handle people. Twice he had displayed his burning sense of justice, first in the impulsive murder and second in the scene with his future wife and her sisters at the well. Without bitterness for his lost position in the royal household, he had turned to the lowly life of a shepherd. He had profited from his mistakes and from the teachings of his priestly father-in-law. He had found a measure of peace in a confident faith. Moses was well prepared.

II

MOSES

THE LEADER

NO STORYBOOK HERO

There are few storybook heroes in the Bible and Moses is certainly not one of them. Would a hero, yielding to a blinding flash of anger, murder an Egyptian as Moses did? No, for we picture a hero as one who easily masters his emotions. And if he does commit a crime, he remains to face his accusers. But Moses fled into the desert.

His panic drove him on, farther and farther from Egypt. He scanned the horizon for pursuers, dreading the sight of chariots sent out by Pharaoh to overtake him. Should they come, he knew his life would be forfeited.

During these hours there was nothing heroic about Moses. Some might even describe him as cowardly. In our codes the only manly thing to do is to accept the consequences of one's action. But in ancient Egypt, there was little justice, little mercy; a man had no chance when the ruler's wrath was aroused. Had Moses remained in Egypt, his life would probably have come to an untimely end. In that case there would have been no liberation from slavery and no Hebrew history as we know it.

Unlike the Bible, which is prone to strip away romantic trappings and present men and women as they really are, with their

11

human failings exposed, we humans are inclined to idealize our heroes. When a man accomplishes something remarkable, we talk about genius. To explain his achievements, we endow him with extraordinary qualities, for otherwise we might suffer too much in our own eyes by comparison with him. It is sometimes hard to accept another's superior accomplishments without ourselves feeling inferior. Romantic hero-making seems to be a device mankind uses to protect its collective ego.

The Scriptures, however, present Moses realistically. For all his greatness—and Moses was indeed a human giant towering over his own people and even over the ages—he often behaved unheroically, as we ourselves might have acted in similar circumstances. But God, who works through human beings as He finds them, used Moses with all his failings of temper, cowardice, and lack of faith—used this man to accomplish His plan for the Exodus.

"I WILL BE WITH YOU"

From the burning bush God spoke to Moses, saying, "Come, I will send you to Pharaoh that you may bring forth my people, the sons of Israel, out of Egypt" (Exod. 3:10).

It was a clear call to greatness and to service, but Moses shrank from such a commission. Accepting it would mean the end of his tranquil life as a shepherd. He would have to leave the solitudes, where his flocks grazed in peace under a limitless sky, for the crowded halls of the royal palace where courtiers competed for power. He had found happiness in the love and companionship of his wife, his two sons, and his wise father-in-law. Their welfare was his chief concern. Why must he assume responsibility for an entire people, with all their burdens? Could he uphold them in their despair or endure their critical murmurings? Moses was convinced that the task to which God called him was impossible.

He cast about for some respectable excuse. Modesty seemed as good as any other.

"Who am I," he asked, "that I should go to Pharaoh, and bring the sons of Israel out of Egypt?" (Exod. 3:11).

It was painfully clear to him who he was—a would-be champion of his people who had already tried to help them and had failed. His humility was really a sense of failure deeply tinged with lack of faith. God's promise cut beneath his self-deceptive modesty to Moses' real need.

"But I will be with you" (Exod. 2:12). God's words rang firm and clear.

Still Moses hesitated before his stupendous task. He must escape from this situation at once. He must find some plausible excuse to decline the commission. Then he remembered one of his weaknesses, a slight one, to be sure, but it might do.

"Oh, my Lord," he answered, "I am not eloquent . . . I am slow of speech and of tongue" (Exod. 4:10).

Perhaps he had a speech impediment such as stuttering. But the Lord, who forever chooses the weak of this world to accomplish His plans, swept away Moses' objection.

"Who has made man's mouth? Who makes him dumb, or deaf, or seeing, or blind? Is it not I, the Lord? Now therefore go, and I will be with your mouth and teach you what you shall speak" (Exod. 4:11-12).

The meaning of this promise came over Moses with a great relief until he found himself not overwhelmed as he feared but buoyed up and confident in the future. Fear, reluctance, the memory of failure, his awareness of his own inadequacies—all were swept away. With God's unlimited power supporting him, he felt his own limited resources to be adequate. Upheld by the power of God, even the weak become strong to accomplish His will. All Moses' later moments of greatness—and there were many of them—stemmed from his complete acceptance of God's call and his trust in God's promise.

HELP ARRIVES

One day on the long journey back to Egypt, Moses saw a solitary figure in the distance slowly trudging toward him over the rough wilderness track. As the man drew closer Moses began to recognize the appearance of his own older brother, Aaron. But would Aaron venture into the wilderness so far from his home in Egypt?

Joyfully the two men met and kissed. Their relief in finding each other was immense. Now Moses realized God had sent Aaron to him. Here was the brother of whom the Lord had said, "And you shall speak to him and put the words in his mouth; and I will be with your mouth and with his mouth, and will teach you what you shall do. He shall speak for you to the people" (Exod. 4:15-16).

By long custom, the elder brother was always given the most important position, yet with rare humility Aaron devoted himself to a secondary role in support of his younger brother. Accepting the subordinate position assigned to him by the Lord, Aaron occupied it with steadfast loyalty to the end, thereby earning an honored place in Hebrew history.

Moses was ready to set forth on his mission. After the anguish of his inner struggle, his mind was at rest. Though he knew he faced bitter strife and an unending battle, he found nothing strange in his father-in-law's blessing, "Go in peace." Moses would not again experience peace as this world knows it, but the treasure of God's peace had been granted to him.

WINNING HIS PEOPLE'S SUPPORT

The first challenge Moses faced upon his return to Egypt was that of winning the confidence of his own people. To them, he was little better than a barely remembered stranger fresh from the desert claiming to be their God-appointed leader. He spoke to them of freedom from slavery, but their ears, so long accustomed to the crack of the taskmaster's whip, could hardly understand the meaning of his words. Somehow Moses must gain their unqualified support and arouse their will to be free, for only with the backing of a united people could he successfully confront Pharaoh.

When he and Aaron faced the assembly of Hebrew elders, Moses saw their unbelief and stubbornness. He also saw apathy and hostility. At this crucial moment how could he rally these men to God's cause?

It is true that the Hebrews were desperate for good news, but they were as wary of easy answers as of groundless hopes. The Bible mentions words spoken and signs performed by Moses and Aaron, and these must have prompted the people to warm to the message. The chief factor, however, in overcoming Hebrew misgivings and arousing faith was surely the direct sincerity with which Moses expressed his convictions. His own strong faith kindled Hebrew hearts.

"And the people believed; and when they heard that the Lord had visited the people of Israel and that he had seen their affliction, they bowed their heads and worshiped" (Exod. 4:31). Through Moses' inspired personality they became aware of the God who would save them.

CONFLICT WITH THE PHARAOH

With the Hebrews behind him, Moses turned to his chief adversary, Pharaoh. Armed with all the might of Egypt and the authority of her ancient religion, Egypt's king stood rigidly opposed to Moses. Theirs is one of the Bible's best-known contests. It was more than a clash between two individuals, or even two peoples, for basically the struggle involved two religions— on the one hand, the Egyptian system which deified the worldly embodiment of oppressive power, and on the other, the Lord, the God of Israel.

In their first audience with Pharaoh, Moses and Aaron made their demand, "Thus says the Lord, the God of Israel, 'Let my people go, that they may hold a feast to me in the wilderness' " (Exod. 5:1).

Contemptuously Pharaoh dismissed his petitioners with the words, "Who is the Lord, that I should heed his voice and let Israel go? I do not know the Lord" (Exod. 5:2). Why should the exalted ruler of Egypt, who believed himself to be a god, listen to some minor deity worshiped by his slaves? His scorn drew a battle line between his own pride and power on one side and, on the other, the eternal Lord who spoke to Moses.

Egypt's king saw Moses' demand as a trumped-up excuse to gain another holiday for his troublesome slaves. To teach them a lesson he commanded, "Get to your burdens" (Exod. 5:4). He instructed his taskmasters to require more and heavier work from the Hebrews, so that they would have no time or energy for agitation or rebellion. Henceforth they must gather their own straw but deliver the same quota of bricks as before. Failure to do so meant beatings.

Anyone who has been imprisoned in a concentration camp knows that there the same policy is used. "Let them work harder," say the authorities, "treat them worse, feed them less. Thus you will break their spirit." It is a cruelly effective strategy.

All that Moses and Aaron did to move the Pharaoh's stubborn resolve is narrated in Exodus. The plagues, their reiterated demand, "Let my people go"—all these merely provoked more obstinate refusals from Egypt's ruler.

Were Moses and the king of Egypt mere figures in a divine chessboard of history where all things are predetermined by God? Are man's actions of no avail? Does man have a free will? There are no simple answers to these questions. One is inclined to see the actions of these Old Testament personalities as the product of their own will. Those, however, for whom the biblical story is fundamental for faith and life see man's freedom of will as a gracious gift from God. Only God is truly free. Our very existence is His gift. Our freedom is a small portion of God's grace and we, like Moses and Pharaoh, are actors in a drama too vast for us to see fully or to understand. In one sense, Moses and the Pharaoh, as they locked in conflict, were free agents of their respective causes. In another sense, they were, by God's design, agents in the fulfillment of His plan.

ESCAPE FROM EGYPT

Discouragement must have weighed heavily upon Moses. The first enthusiasm of his people began to wane. Though the inhabitants of Egypt watched in horror all the signs he performed, Pharaoh continued his refusal to let the Hebrews go. Under pressure, he behaved as every tyrant does, promising whatever is asked, but going back on his word as soon as pressure is relaxed. Undismayed by these failures, and calmly relying on divine command, Moses prepared to lead the Hebrews out of Egypt. At this moment, with all the odds against him, his real greatness emerges.

On the night of the Passover, God took all the firstborn of Egypt, but the angel of death passed by the Hebrew dwellings, where blood had been spattered above the doors and on the doorposts as a sign that these enslaved people had already paid their sacrifice. The Scriptures understand this event as an act of God's justice, a justice that worked two ways, punishing the Egyptians while freeing the Hebrews.

The group of slaves which left Egypt was fairly large. From the passage stating that two midwives served the Hebrews, their number might be estimated as small. But others besides the descendants of Jacob were in the multitude led by Moses. In one passage, the people of the Exodus are described as "a mixed multitude" (12:38), meaning, no doubt, a group composed of several racial groups. Here the Bible shows that God's Chosen People were not one race as we understand the term today, but a group transcending race and nationality.

Not by the easy route out of Egypt, the old coastal "Road of the Sea," did Moses lead his people to freedom. There is no direct highway from slavery to freedom. Instead Moses led them inland toward the wilderness, where they camped beside the Sea of Reeds.

Suddenly, in the direction from which they had come, they saw a dust cloud on the horizon. Every man knew what it meant— at the last moment the Pharaoh had changed his mind once more and had sent his chariot corps to overtake them. Their wives and their children, their old parents and their youths, both the strong and the weak—all were trapped between the sea and the oncoming chariots. In this hopeless plight, they gave in to despair. Moses had brought them here, so they turned on him with bitter accusations.

"Is it because there are no graves in Egypt that you have taken us away to die in the wilderness?" they cried to him. "What have you done to us, in bringing us out of Egypt? . . . For it would have been better for us to serve the Egyptians than to die in the wilderness" (Exod. 14:12).

Moses knew how his people felt, for not many years before he himself had fled in terror of a personal calamity. But now, while the Egyptian chariots thundered on, Moses rallied his demoralized people.

"Fear not, stand firm, and see the salvation of the Lord, which he will work for you today; for the Egyptians whom you see today, you shall never see again. The Lord will fight for you, and you have only to be still" (Exod. 14:13-14).

The record of what followed can be interpreted in two ways. Some natural phenomenon may have caused the waters of the sea to recede temporarily. Seizing this opportunity, the Hebrews could have escaped dry-shod over the exposed sea bottom. When the waves surged back, the pursuing Egyptians would be caught and drowned. According to another view, the Hebrews may have waded easily through the marshes of the Sea of Reeds in which the heavy Egyptian armor and chariots would become hopelessly mired. Whichever theory one prefers, the incredible outcome of the event was the same—the Egyptian chariots were defeated but Israel was saved.

In gratitude for their deliverance, the women of Israel led by Miriam the prophetess, sister of Moses and Aaron, praised God to whom belonged the glory for their mighty salvation:

Sing to the Lord, for he has triumphed gloriously; the horse and his rider he has thrown into the sea.   Exod. 15:21

IN THE WILDERNESS

Freed from fear of pursuit, the Hebrews continued their journey into the wilderness. Moses led them along part of the trade route connecting Egypt and Arabia and southward along the road to the turquoise and copper mines worked by slaves for the Egyptians in the Sinai Peninsula. Long ago as a boy in the royal palace, Moses may have heard tales of officials who had traveled along these roads. Perhaps their information now stood him in good stead as he led Israel deeper into the wilderness.

The people were far from ready to face enemies or to wage war. They needed to live apart for a while so that they might be forged into a nation. Like Moses himself only a few years before, these wanderers needed to experience the solitude of the wilderness where a man can contemplate something larger than himself. In the desert the Hebrews were alone with their God.

HIS RELIGIOUS CONTRIBUTION

Sitting wearily in his tent at sunset, after the problems of each day had been met, Moses must often have wondered how the whole enterprise would end. How could he transform the mixed group of slaves who had followed him from Egypt into the unified people of God? Had he but known it, he was succeeding remarkably well, for he was bringing to his people three unifying elements: a definite religious faith, a definite law, and a definite worship.

Many books have been written about the origin of the religion Moses taught his people. Some believe that he built upon fragments of tribal memory learned in his youth. Others say that he heard of the one God, Yahweh, from his wise father-in-law, the Kenite priest Reuel. Still others assert that the Book of Exodus projects backward into the period of Moses the more developed form of Hebrew religion existing when the book itself was written.

Despite elements of truth in these theories, the Scriptures are clear about this point: the essence of Israel's religion, which forged a group of rebellious slaves into a covenant people under

God, was divinely inspired and expressly given by God to His people through one man, Moses. Though the patriarchs had played their part, the maker of Israel, the people of God, was definitely Moses.

"I am the Lord your God, who brought you out of the land of Egypt, out of the house of bondage. You shall have no other gods before me" (Exod. 20:2-3). This pronouncement of God, given to Moses and relayed to his people, is precise dogma. We of the modern world dislike dogma just as the Hebrews did in the days of Moses. It is disturbing to be told officially that you must believe with all your heart and unconditionally trust the one spiritual God of the universe. In the Scriptures this is the central issue of faith.

The Hebrews resisted dogma, demanding that Aaron make them a golden idol of a calf from the precious metal of their jewelry. In the insecurity of the wilderness it would remind them of the Egyptian gods they had left behind. Aaron did not exactly introduce a new deity, for the calf represented Yahweh who had brought them out of the land of Egypt. Aaron only tried to put in visible form the One who is above and beyond all forms. He tried to tie God to an idolatrous throne seat in the form of an animal. Thus, the people would be able to control their God. Learning of his people's idol worship, Moses became so angry that he broke the stone tablets of the law. Would they never understand the majestic holiness and the otherness of their Lord?

THE LAW

The definite law which Moses gave his people was revealed to him on Mount Sinai while the Hebrews waited in the valley below. Again, there are many indications that the Ten Commandments, and the later laws of Moses, have their roots in older laws long observed in the lands of the Fertile Crescent. The law of Hammurabi and other legal texts of this area are much older than the Exodus. Moses, with a background which had exposed him to a broader world than that of most of his people, had assuredly absorbed many legal ideas. Then, as today, cultures mingled. But Moses had something new, something unique to give his people. He taught them a law that is completely God-centered. It provides for no king, no omnipotent state, no priestly caste, no power of the created world. This law, with all the precision of its commandments, is God's will.

HEBREW WORSHIP

Dogma, law, and finally worship—these were Moses' legacy to the Hebrews. He gave them the definite ceremonies first described in Exodus 25. Some of us like to think that worship is good only if it is simple. The forms Moses prescribed are not simple, nor did they allow much scope for personal freedom of expression. Homage paid to God was to be precise, with all its details spelled out. Even if some of the present text describing worship reflects later, more elaborate ritual, the core indicates enough of the complexity of Mosaic ceremonial to establish that the form was already there.

MOSES' LOVE FOR HIS PEOPLE

After the people's disobedience in making their calf idol of gold, the Lord planned to extinguish Israel so that He could make a new beginning with Moses as a second Noah. "I have seen this people," declared the Lord, "and behold, it is a stiff-necked people; now therefore let me alone, that my wrath may burn hot against them and I may consume them; but of you I will make a great nation" (Exod. 32:9).

Moses was torn with compassion for his people. As a leader who loved his followers, he accepted full responsibility for their actions. He felt himself deeply involved in their destiny. Passionately he prayed to the Lord to spare the faithless Hebrews.

"O Lord," he prayed, "why does thy wrath burn hot against thy people, whom thou hast brought forth out of the land of Egypt with great power and with a mighty hand? . . . Turn from thy fierce wrath, and repent of this evil against thy people" (Exod. 32:11-12).

Deep in his heart Moses knew that if he loved the people surely the Lord, who had chosen them, freed them, and preserved them through many dangers—surely the Lord loved them more. The same God who demands obedience to His laws is also the God of loving forgiveness. He is indeed the God of salvation. Moses' prayer was answered with mercy, for he interceded with One who is far more willing to give than men are to receive.

MOSES' DEATH

Moses had served God faithfully. He had led the people through the desert, following the pillar of fire by night and the pillar of cloud by day. Sometimes he cajoled them, often he threatened. Through all their dangers he upheld their spirits and welded them into a nation. But this great man was not permitted to enter the Promised Land.

"And the Lord said to Moses that very day, 'Ascend this mountain of the Abarim, Mount Nebo, which is in the land of Moab, opposite Jericho; and view the land of Canaan, which I give to the people of Israel for a possession; and die on the mountain which you ascend . . . because you broke faith with me in the midst of the people of Israel . . . in the wilderness of Zin; because you did not revere me as holy in the midst of the people of Israel. For you shall see the land before you; but you shall not go there" (Deut. 32:48-52).

What had Moses done to deserve this punishment? One day

in the wilderness of Zin he had assumed the role of God. The Bible seems to indicate that in a momentary loss of faith, he took for himself credit that belonged to God when he struck the rock and water gushed out for the thirsty Hebrews.

The death of Moses at the gate of the Promised Land is deeply symbolic. Complete perfection or unadulterated success is not given to men. Creatures as we are, everything we do is stamped with our attributes as men occupying a station below God.

"So Moses the servant of the Lord died there in the land of Moab, according to the word of the Lord, and he buried him in the valley . . . but no man knows the place of his burial to this day" (Deut. 34:5-6).

Moses literally disappeared from the sight of his people. No pilgrims visit his grave nor can a monument be erected there, for his burial place is unknown. But he left behind his own monument in a faith that has produced three world religions: Judaism, Christianity, and Islam. His legacy was an organized society, the covenant people of Israel. Christians revere his memory, for he laid the basic foundation for the teachings of Christ.

Moreover, Christians find in many aspects of Moses' life a foreshadowing of Christ. Both appeared as helpless babies, the one concealed among bulrushes, the other lying in a manger. Moses left a king's palace to become champion of his people, while of Jesus it was said that "though he was rich, yet for your sake he became poor" (II Cor. 8:9). As Moses was mistrusted by his own people, so Jesus "came to his own home, and his own people received him not" (John 1:11). Moses delivered the Hebrews from bondage by teaching them the will of God. In a deeper sense Christ delivers mankind in the same way. Thus Moses, whom "God sent as both ruler and deliverer" (Acts 7:35), stands at the beginning of Hebrew history as the symbol of the One who, in the fullness of time, was to appear.

III

J O S H U A
THE CONQUEROR

TRAINING FOR LEADERSHIP

The great leader of the Hebrews and his young assistant were descending Mount Sinai with the two stone tables of the law. Joshua, who had been privileged to accompany his master beyond the point where the elders were commanded to stop and wait, had been the closest to Moses when God gave him the law. Now as they returned to camp, Joshua listened intently to a far-off sound as of shouting. Man of war that he was, Joshua sensed danger to the people he and Moses served. Had enemies attacked them while Moses communed with God on the holy mountain?

"There is a noise of war in the camp" (Exod. 32:17), cried Joshua, preparing to rush down to defend the camp.

But Moses sensed a different note in the clamor and knew a deeper threat faced him and his people.

"It is not the sound of shouting for victory, or the sound of the cry of defeat, but the sound of singing that I hear" (Exod. 32:18). The unfaithful people were dancing and making merry around the golden calf, the idol Aaron had made at their insistence.

25

After this crisis was met, Joshua continued to stand beside Moses, aiding him in both trials and triumphs. Moses not only admitted his young follower into the tent of meeting where Moses talked with God, but he honored the young man by leaving him in charge of the tent.

"When Moses entered the tent, the pillar of cloud would descend and stand at the door of the tent, and the Lord would speak with Moses. . . . Thus the Lord used to speak to Moses face to face, as a man speaks to his friend. When Moses turned again to the camp, his servant Joshua, the son of Nun, a young man, did not depart from the tent" (Exod. 33:9, 11).

At the right hand of every leader of a great enterprise there is need of a faithful assistant, trained to carry on his master's work. Such a follower will be influenced by the spirit of his master, often to such an extent that the younger man may imitate the greater personality and see things only with the eyes of his master. Such an uncreative follower will lack the ability to meet new situations as they arise.

In the case of Moses and Joshua the danger of slavish following did not arise, for Joshua was more than an accompanying shadow. Tradition pictures him as a militant man of action, endowed with vision, and strong in faith.

THE AMALEKITES ATTACK

Joshua's reputation as a military leader was won in his battle against the Amalekites. A band of these nomadic marauders attacked the Hebrews while they were encamped in the wilderness at Rephidim near Mount Sinai. This was the first armed resistance Israel had encountered since leaving Egypt and it might have thrown the people into such confusion that they would never have recovered. The success of their journey to freedom hung in the balance at Rephidim. Israel had not yet trained a military force to repel armed attacks, nor had the people become sufficiently united to withstand defeat.

In this moment of peril, Moses turned to Joshua, commissioning his young assistant to act. "Choose for us men, and go out, fight with Amalek" (Exod. 17:9).

Joshua, so suddenly made a military commander, carefully surveyed the Hebrew ranks and chose from them the strongest and most reliable men for this crucial military test.

During the ensuing encounter, Moses stood on top of a hill overlooking the battlefield. Above his head he raised his sign of office, the banner of Israel, the rod of God. As long as he held it aloft, the Hebrews prevailed, but when he lowered it, the Amalekites gained the upper hand. When Moses grew tired, Aaron brought a stone for him to sit on and with the help of Hur, one of the leading Hebrews, supported Moses' arms on either side so that he could continue to hold the rod until the battle was won.

Thus with the combined efforts of Moses, Joshua, and the valiant men of Israel, their first foreign enemy was successfully routed.

No longer was Joshua regarded merely as Moses' assistant; the victory at Rephidim earned him acclaim as a military commander. Moses, perceiving that Joshua's outstanding ability guaranteed the continuation of God's plan for the Chosen People, made him the keeper of tradition and memory.

"And the Lord said to Moses, 'Write this as a memorial in a book and recite it in the ears of Joshua . . .'" (Exod. 17:14).

BACK TO EGYPT! CRIED THE PEOPLE

Later, when the wandering Hebrews reached the southern border of the Promised Land, Moses sent advance scouts to spy out conditions there. They returned carrying a huge bunch of ripe grapes on a pole and also some pomegranates and figs. To them, after their years in the wilderness, Canaan seemed a veritable paradise, a land of milk and honey indeed. But the men also brought the discouraging report that "the people who dwell in the land are strong, and the cities are fortified and very large" (Num. 13:28).

The thought of invading this land seemed so foolhardy to the spies that they tried to dissuade the people by saying, "All the people that we saw in it are men of great stature . . . and we seemed to ourselves like grasshoppers, and so we seemed to them" (Num. 13:32-33).

Grasshoppers confronting giants!—the idea so frightened the Hebrews that they cried, "Would that we had died in the land of Egypt! Or that we had died in this wilderness! Why does the Lord bring us into this land, to fall by the sword? Our wives and our little ones will become a prey; would it not be better for us to go back to Egypt?" (Num. 14:2-3)

At this moment when the people's morale reached such a low point that they had begun to choose a leader to take them back to Egypt, Joshua came forward. With him was his comrade Caleb. Both of them had accompanied the other spies, but Joshua and Caleb had seen the land through the eyes of faith, not fear.

"The land, which we passed through to spy it out," they declared, "is an exceedingly good land. If the Lord delights in us, he will bring us into this land and give it to us, a land which flows with milk and honey. Only, do not rebel against the Lord; and do not fear the people of the land . . . the Lord is with us" (Num. 14:7-9).

ORDINATION TO LEADERSHIP

Joshua knew that Israel's failure of nerve came from her lack of faith in God's power to preserve her. Would the people never learn to trust in the Lord's promises? Would they never see, as

Joshua did, that all Israel's hardships were gradually uniting a ragged horde of slaves into the disciplined people of God? In his own person Joshua personified confidence in the Lord.

These qualities of strength and trust led Moses to choose Joshua as his successor. No one was better equipped to assume responsibility as leader or to bring the Hebrews at last into the Promised Land. Over the years he had proven himself a dependable servant, and his natural courage rallied men behind him in battle. His practical vision and military imagination were crowned by a deeply spiritual nature.

In the ancient ceremony of the laying on of hands, which has been, and still is, the sign of transfer of office and spiritual power, Moses made Joshua his successor, thus fulfilling the Lord's command.

"Take Joshua the son of Nun, a man in whom is the spirit, and lay your hand upon him; cause him to stand before Eleazar the priest and all the congregation, and you shall commission him in their sight. You shall invest him with some of your authority, that all the congregation of the people of Israel may obey" (Num. 27:18-20).

In ordination scenes like this, the continuity of a religious community is guaranteed. Personal pride and self-seeking lose their grip upon a man to whom truth is handed on in a chain from leader to leader and from generation to generation. In such a context a man sees himself humbly as a servant in the community in which God deals with man.

When Joshua assumed leadership he received a clear promise of God's help. "Moses my servant is dead; now therefore arise, go over this Jordan, you and all this people, into the land which I am giving to them . . . as I was with Moses, so I will be with you; I will not fail you or forsake you. Be strong and of good courage; for you shall cause this people to inherit the land. . . . be not frightened, neither be dismayed; for the Lord your God is with you wherever you go" (Josh. 1:2, 5-6, 9).

CANAAN RIPE FOR INVASION

The political disorder Joshua found in the Promised Land of Canaan is reflected in some of the more than three hundred Tell el 'Amarna Letters. These date from 1370 to 1353 B.C., a century or so before Joshua reached Canaan. Written on clay tablets and recovered by archaeologists from the royal archives at Amarna, the letters deal with the foreign affairs of Pharaoh Amenhotep IV, better known as Ikhnaton. This king's interest in religion led him to introduce a form of monotheism into Egypt. As a result of his efforts to reform religion, he neglected political and military affairs in his empire, which extended north of Canaan into Syria and beyond. Inevitably, with Egypt's outposts poorly defended, rapacious invaders closed in, plundering the countryside.

Among the invaders were the Semitic people called 'Apiru who raided and even captured cities under Egyptian rule. Habdu-Heba, the Egyptian governor of Jerusalem whose letters are among the Tell el 'Amarna documents, wrote frantically to his superiors in Egypt saying that his garrison was "like a ship in the midst of the sea" surrounded by invading 'Apiru. "The 'Apiru are taking the cities of the king. No ruler remains to the king, my lord; all are lost." In another letter, the Canaanite ruler of Shechem, Lab'ayu, is taken to task by his Egyptian overlords for permitting the 'Apiru to settle on the land.

Though these writers do not seem to be referring to Joshua and his Hebrew warriors, their letters do reveal some of the reasons why Joshua found the Promised Land ripe for invasion. In some cases he was able to form alliances with Semitic groups that were considered relatives of the Hebrews, though they had not shared their desert experience. At Shechem he met no resistance. The Semitic raiders who for a century or more had harassed Canaan doubtless prepared the way of Joshua's invasion.

From the sea came new invaders among whom were the Philistines. For these people Canaan was later named "Palestine." The Egyptians of the 19th Dynasty succeeded in checking the Philistines and bottling them up in a small, coastal area of southern Canaan.

By this time Egypt was exhausted by her wars and Canaan, where no major power held single sway, lay open to Joshua's attack. Far from being inhabited by "giants," as they had seemed to the spies, the land was occupied by a people disunited and demoralized by political upheavals. Once-bristling defenses had been neglected, and Semitic tribes related to the Hebrews were already established in Canaan.

A RIVER TO CROSS

Another obstacle still barred the Hebrews from the Promised Land. The waters of the Jordan River flowed between them and the land at which they gazed with longing. It was now harvest time, when the river overflowed its banks, making even its fords impassable (Josh. 3:15). How could Joshua and his people gain the opposite bank?

Trusting in the Lord's promise, Joshua gave orders to advance. Obediently the people approached the Jordan and saw to their amazement that it had stopped flowing, for "the waters coming down from above stood and rose up in a heap far off" (Josh. 3:16). With the flow of water blocked to the north of them, the people of Israel made their way across the still-damp stones lying in the dry river bed. In modern times landslides and geological changes caused by earthquakes have sometimes been known to block the Jordan River for considerable periods, making possible a dry crossing below the dam.

The Hebrew men selected twelve stones from the river with

which to build a monument to their safe crossing. This monument, symbolizing the unity of the twelve tribes as they entered the Promised Land, was erected at Gilgal. Here, while the men were away on wars of conquest, the women, children, and old people set up their camp in relative safety.

JERICHO FALLS

Spies had already been sent on to Jericho to observe its fortifications and estimate its available manpower. The men had been instructed to find a way to capture this stronghold. In Jericho they found lodging and a good source of information at the house of a woman named Rahab. The Bible translations call her a harlot, doubtless because she was connected with the sexual practices of the Canaanite religion.

While in the city the spies' mission was discovered by the king of Jericho, who sent to Rahab, ordering her, "Bring forth the men that have come to you, who entered your house; for they have come to search out all the land" (Josh. 2:3).

But Rahab hid her boarders under stalks of flax drying upon the flat roof. As soon as the king's search party left her house, which was built against the city wall, she let the spies down from her window with a rope, so that they landed outside the city and returned safely to Joshua.

Encouraged by the report from Jericho, Joshua advanced upon the city. Before he led his troops against it, he ordered all men to be circumcised. The original group which left Egypt had been circumcised, but the men now of fighting age, born during the forty years in the wilderness, had not undergone the ritual. By applying this covenant sign, the Hebrew warriors expressed their belonging to the covenant God.

Archaeologists, digging into the remains of Jericho, have proved that this ancient stronghold with its massive walls had already been destroyed before the Hebrews appeared. What Joshua's men probably found was a small fortress built upon the ruins of the old city.

The tradition of Jericho's siege and fall is preserved in the colorful story of warriors marching for seven days around the city, accompanied by priests blowing ram's-horn trumpets before the ark. At the climax of the siege, "As soon as the people heard the sound of the trumpet, the people raised a great shout, and the wall fell down flat, so that the people went up into the city . . . and they took the city" (Josh. 6:20).

To Joshua, the fall of Jericho proved that his men could conquer Canaanite fortifications. If the very sound of the priests' trumpets destroyed a city's resistance, the time was ripe for Hebrew conquest.

JOSHUA'S CAMPAIGNS

Joshua led his victorious troops westward from Jericho toward Ai-Bethel, where by clever ambush and diversion he won a victory that drove a wedge into the center of Canaan.

The territory north of the wedge, in the area of Shechem, was already held by the 'Apiru, who apparently posed no threat to the Hebrews, so Joshua next turned south. Hearing of Joshua's military success, the Hivites living in Gibeon and its surrounding cities became fearful for their safety. By lying and false pretenses they succeeded in extracting a peace treaty from the Hebrews, who soon discovered that they had been tricked. Nevertheless the Hebrews, because they had sealed the treaty with an oath in the name of the Lord, the God of Israel, felt bound to their new allies, the unreliable people of Gibeon.

Farther south the five Amorite kings of Jerusalem, Hebron, Jarmuth, Lachish, and Eglon formed an alliance against the invaders. Near Gibeon the kings hurled their forces against Israel.

In describing this battle, the Book of Joshua quotes a fragment of an ancient song once contained in the lost Book of Jashar.

Then spoke Joshua to the Lord in the day when the Lord gave the Amorites over to the men of Israel. . . .

> "Sun, stand thou still at Gibeon,
> and thou Moon in the valley of Aijalon."

> And the sun stood still, and the moon stayed,
> until the nation took vengeance on their enemies.

Is this not written in the Book of Jashar? The sun stayed in the midst of heaven, and did not hasten to go down for about a whole day. There has been no day like it before or since, when the Lord hearkened to the voice of a man; for the Lord fought for Israel.   Josh. 10:12-14

Attempts are often made to explain this miracle of a lengthened day. Some people believe that the writer of the Book of Joshua may have misquoted the fragment of ancient verse. Other people point to scientific theories of cosmic catastrophes that would support the biblical text. But scientific thinking did not exist for those who first told this story of a sun that stood still so that the people of God might prevail. The story dramatizes a vivid experience that the Lord of the universe was on Israel's side in the midst of battle.

The third phase of Joshua's campaign began after the south of Canaan was captured and the Hebrew columns marched north. No resistance was reported except in the far north, where Joshua defeated the alliance of northern Canaanite kings by the waters of Merom. The way now lay open to the mighty city of Hazor near the headwaters of the Jordan. According to archaeological excavations in the rich remains of Hazor, the city was one of the best fortified and most densely populated of the whole area. But

it too fell to Joshua's battle-hardened and disciplined veterans.
The conquest was over; Canaan was won.

DIVISION OF THE LAND

Beginning with the thirteenth chapter of the Book of Joshua,
the distribution of the conquered land to each tribe and clan is
carefully recorded. The account gives the impression of a modern
registry of deeds. Joshua received an inheritance for himself and
his family: "By command of the Lord they gave him the city
which he asked, Timnath-serah in the hill country of Ephraim; and
he rebuilt the city, and settled in it" (Josh. 19:50).

After the tent of meeting was set up at Shiloh, lots were cast
there for the lands to be assigned to the remaining seven tribes.
The casting of lots was not to the ancient Hebrews, nor to the
early Christians (Acts 1:26), an act of irresponsible gambling, but
an act of faith in the real presence of God operating in the midst
of His people.

THE ACCOMPLISHMENTS OF JOSHUA

From the moment when Joshua gave the signal to advance
across the Jordan, his days had been filled with one crisis after
another. He had studied each situation carefully and devised some
brilliant military plans. As a leader giving orders, he was sure of
himself. Now in the relative tranquility of his new home in
Timnath-serah where he was building up, not destroying, he could
look back upon the events of his life. What had he accomplished
for his people?

Unlike the modern reader of his exploits, Joshua did not
question the means by which he conquered. Total destruction of
an enemy whose religious practices were abhorrent seemed only
right to him. Such cruelty he accepted as necessary in the painful

process of welding a group of almost stone-age tribesmen into a nation. As he battled to gain for his people a place to live, he had no time for laughter or lightness. His personality is portrayed without many of the attractive human traits of such other leaders as Moses, Saul, or David. Obsessed as he was with the seriousness of his task, Joshua pursued the terrible business of war until he was finally victorious.

Had he not led a horde of seminomads out of the wilderness and made them masters of the hill country of Canaan? It was an astonishing feat. Instead of wandering hungrily from oasis to oasis in the arid reaches of the desert, the Hebrews now could build walled towns, plow fertile fields, and in peace gather fruit from their own orchards and vineyards. Joshua could reflect that the charge entrusted to him by Moses and the God of Israel had been fulfilled.

But one question remained. Would the tribal federation Joshua had formed be able to keep what they had won? They had conquered in the strength of their faith in the Lord. But temptations to abandon their covenant faith in favor of the foreign gods of Canaan were a constant threat. Would Israel be able to win the land of Canaan to their own faith? As so often in history or in personal life, the great question is not the conquest but the holding, or as the New Testament put it: the great question is not conversion, but remaining faithful.

RENEWAL OF THE COVENANT AT SHECHEM

Joshua's story concludes with a great assembly of the tribes of Israel at the sanctuary at Shechem, where the people presented themselves to God. After reminding them of the wonderful works God had performed for them, Joshua challenged his people in forceful words to renew the allegiance they had once pledged to Him at Sinai.

"Now therefore fear the Lord, and serve him in sincerity and in faithfulness, . . ." he exhorted them. "And if you be unwilling to serve the Lord, choose this day whom you will serve, whether the gods your father served in the region beyond the River, or the gods of the Amorites in whose land you dwell" (Josh. 24:14-15).

Aware of the powerful temptations his people faced, Joshua added the announcement of his own personal decision, throwing the weight of his authority behind the cause of the Lord he had followed so long: "As for me and my house, we will serve the Lord" (Josh. 24:15).

The people responded with one voice. "Far be it from us that we should forsake the Lord, to serve other gods"; they shouted, "for it is the Lord our God who brought us and our fathers up from the land of Egypt. . . . Therefore we also will serve the Lord, for he is our God" (Josh. 24:16-18). The covenant of the wilderness was remembered and renewed in the Land of Promise. From Moses to Joshua, from Sinai to Shechem, the covenant held the people to their past, to one another, and to God. It would become the vital link that bound and sustained them through a stormy history.

Joshua's contribution to his people is expressed in this final estimate of his work, "And Israel served the Lord all the days of Joshua, and all the days of the elders who outlived Joshua and had known all the work which the Lord did for Israel" (Josh. 24:31).

IV

S A M S O N
THE HERO

HIS BIRTH

Manoah and his wife were a childless couple of the tribe of Dan, dwelling in the town of Zorah, halfway between Jerusalem and the sea. They lived during the unsettled period after the conquest when the so-called "judges" ruled the Hebrews. One day an angel of the Lord appeared to Manoah's wife with the happy tidings that she would bear a son.

She listened carefully while the messenger gave her explicit directions about leading a disciplined life. She was to taste no wine or other fermented drink and to eat nothing unclean. The reason for these special prohibitions was that her son was to be a Nazirite, a man dedicated to special service under God.

"And," declared the angel concerning the son to be born to her, "he shall begin to deliver Israel from the hand of the Philistines" (Judg. 13:5).

The Hebrew religion contained dietary laws and enjoined bodily discipline, but the body was not regarded with suspicion. As God created the fruit of the vine and all manner of food, the Hebrews believed it their sacred duty to enjoy the good things He gave them. This same attitude applied to the joys of the family. If a man went into the wilderness to be alone with his God, then it was only for a time, not a lifelong state of being. There was no extreme asceticism, except in the case of the Nazirites, individuals under special vows.

Samson, the child to be born, was to be such a consecrated man, set apart for all to see, for no razor was to cut the hair of his head. Older Bible translators used the term "Vowed to God," because often a Nazirite was promised to God's service by his mother's vow before birth, as in the case of Samson. His particular calling was to free his fellow Israelites from the Philistines who for forty years had continued to harass them.

Manoah did not know what to make of his wife's good news. A sense of his own inadequacy assailed him. How could he bring up a son with such a destiny? All he could do was to plead, "O, Lord, I pray thee, let the man of God whom thou didst send come again to us, and teach us what we are to do with the boy that will be born" (Judg. 13:8).

When the messenger appeared again, Manoah wanted to offer him customary hospitality. But learning that he was indeed an angel of God, Manoah became frightened, believing that he had looked upon that which no man can see and live. "We shall surely die," he cried to his wife, "for we have seen God" (Judg. 13:22).

His wife, more practical and less emotional than her husband, sensibly argued that the Lord would not have promised them a son if He intended them to die.

In due time Samson was born, the only son of parents who were no longer young. While it was almost impossible for such a boy not to be spoiled by doting parents, they had such high religious hopes for their son and lived in such strict piety, that the child Samson must often have felt a keen sense of rebellion against all they stood for.

THE TIME OF THE JUDGES

Manoah and his wife brought up their promised son in an Israel that was little more than a confederation of tribes lacking a central administration. After Joshua's death, Shechem remained the annual meeting place of the tribes. Attempts by Gideon and Abimelech to weld them more firmly together under a central government had failed. Until the appearance of Samuel and Saul, Israel's only rulers were the "judges," charismatic individuals who arose from time to time to deal with special crises. Though they were regarded as leaders sent by God, their service was limited to a definite emergency, for the tribes rejected the idea of a strong ruler over them all.

The Book of Judges, after narrating in strong colors the events of this cruel, reckless age, sums up the period in a closing sentence, "In those days there was no king in Israel; every man did what was right in his own eyes" (Judg. 21:25). Because the Shechem confederacy could not fully unite the tribes, it gradually became clear that a monarchy was necessary. But this remained far in the future while Samson was growing up in Dan on the border of Philistine territory.

CULTURAL BACKWARDNESS

As a boy Samson may have played in the rubble of destroyed cities or tested his growing strength by moving some of the great stones once built into defensive walls. Archaeological diggings in Palestine reveal that the invading Hebrew tribes destroyed many large cities, but did not rebuild them to their original strength. A people who had lived in tents for a generation did not know how to erect a well-fortified city or even how to live in one.

Samson observed that his Philistine neighbors to the south

seemed always to have the upper hand. Their farming tools were more effective and their weapons more powerful than those of the Hebrews. The explanation is simple, for Israelite skills and methods were still those of the bronze age, while the Philistines had already advanced to the iron age with its superior economic and military advantage. No wonder that Israel was given "into the hand of the Philistines for forty years" (Judg. 13:1). Even in the use of domesticated animals, the Hebrew tribes were far behind the peoples surrounding them.

"YOU SHALL HAVE NO OTHER GODS BEFORE ME"

Israel was eager to learn from her neighbors, even in religious matters. When challenged by Joshua at Shechem, the people had chosen to worship not the Canaanite gods but the God of their fathers, the God of the Sinai covenant. As time went on, however, and the people exchanged their nomadic life for an agricultural one, the religious practices of their neighbors became less repulsive to them. A growing laxity began to eat away at Israel's religious life.

A mixing of religions was constantly taking place throughout the entire region—Mesopotamia, Asia Minor, Syria, and Canaan—for the nations of the Fertile Crescent were never tightly closed entities with stable borders. Peoples borrowed from each other and learned from each other, recognizing similarities between their own gods and the gods of their neighbors. Traders' caravans freely carried legends and myths across all boundaries.

Samson must have been aware, at an early age, that the God his parents worshiped was not the god of the Canaanites, who followed a nature religion centering around an epic of the life-death-life cycle of Baal. Tablets inscribed with this epic were found in 1929 at Ras Shamra, the site of the ancient Canaanite city of Ugarit, on the coast of northern Syria. The tablets, assigned to a period before 1350 B.C., give important evidence about Canaanite belief and worship.

In the Canaanite religious imagination the supreme god was El and his consort was Asherah. Below them ruled Baal, lord of lords, creator, god of weather, and giver of rain and fertility. Mot, god of the summer drought, persecutes Baal, kills him, and carries him to the underworld. Baal's consort, the violent and brutal war goddess Anath, pursues Mot and kills him. Then Baal is resurrected and again enthroned as the creator of all earthly fertility. The nature cycle then begins again.

Baal's story from the Ras Shamra tablets is an example of the nature religions prevalent in Canaan. The seasons rotate; the gods are personifications of the cycle of the year. This religion moves between the despair of death and the joy of returning life. It features the violent abandonment of man in the sexual experience and dwells on the continuation of life out of apparent death.

Nature religions have contributed to a widespread misinterpretation of religion. For instance, the Christian Easter could easily be demeaned into a spring rite by saying that as barren trees sprout their new leaves each spring, so Jesus Christ rose from the dead. But this interpretation is a perversion of the Christian message. Viewing the Jewish Passover merely as a spring festival, without keeping its definite association with the Exodus, is a similar perversion. In the Bible, God is not the symbol of the eternal cycle of the seasons. He is far more than that—He is Lord of the universe. The natural processes are but one part of His creation. The nature religions give believers a new chance every year, but in the Judeo-Christian tradition, a deed performed is *done*—a part of human history, not natural process—and only divine forgiveness can alter the consequences.

Baal worship for the Canaanite farmer of Samson's day was a means of ensuring good crops. This nature religion had about the same function as fertilization of the soil has for the modern farmer. In order to raise crops as good as their neighbors', many of the Hebrews adopted Baal worship, afraid to risk offending a god who might give them a good harvest. Thus, though they still regarded Yahweh as their chief deity, they began to add the gods of their neighbors.

Yahweh, however, is a "jealous" God. Today when we do not consider jealousy a virtue, it is difficult to understand what the Hebrews meant by this term. In contemporary English the closest meaning is that Yahweh is exclusive. He permits no division of loyalty. "I am the Lord your God, who brought you out of the land of Egypt, out of the house of bondage. You shall have no other gods before me" (Deut. 5:6-7). Israel struggled throughout her history to increase her zeal for Yahweh alone, to purify her relationship with her one God.

"TO THE LORD I WILL SING . . . THE GOD OF ISRAEL"

Not long before Samson was born, Israel won a brilliant military victory. It was celebrated in a magnificent ode which may have stirred the imagination of the youthful Samson, for it is a story of heroism and of faith in the Lord.

The action took place when a woman named Deborah was "judge" of Israel. The Canaanites were oppressing the Hebrews when Deborah summoned Barak, an outstanding military leader, to rally the tribes and lead them against the Canaanites near Megiddo. This strategic fortress controlled a narrow pass through the mountains where the main highway between Egypt and Mesopotamia ran. Megiddo was in Canaanite hands and defended by Sisera, a Canaanite chieftain. After a fierce engagement beside the Kishon River, the Hebrew tribes led by Deborah and Barak defeated Sisera.

Deborah's song of victory, in Judges 5, gives a poetic account of the encounter, while at the same time expressing Israel's faith in capsule form. It declares God to be the God of history. Israel is Israel only through her obedience to the Lord. Not by virtue of his family or race does a person become an active member of the covenant community, but by obedience in the present to the Lord God of Israel.

Would Samson be able to meet the challenge of his day in this faith? While defeating the Philistines, would Samson strengthen Israel's loyalty to her God?

HIS PHILISTINE BRIDE

Samson was known from the first as a rebellious, impulsive man of huge strength and courage. The first story about him concerns a young woman of the Philistine town of Timnah. Samson fell in love with her and demanded of his father, "Get her for me; for she pleases me well" (Judg. 14:3).

His parents argued that because he was destined to liberate the Hebrews from Philistine domination, it was wrong for him to take a daughter of the enemy as his wife. With complete disregard for his parents' advice or for their religious convictions, Samson stubbornly persisted in his demand. As usual, his father gave in to the headstrong youth.

Once on his way to Timnah, a young lion had blocked the road, but with his powerful arms Samson fearlessly "tore the lion asunder as one tears a kid" (Judg. 14:6). Later, passing by the same place, Samson saw that a swarm of bees had settled in the lion's carcass. Pleased with himself, he scraped out the honey and ate it as he walked along.

When he married the Philistine woman, thirty young men were invited to the week-long celebration. During the festivities Samson made a bet with these Philistines that they would not be able to solve his riddle,

Out of the eater came something to eat.
Out of the strong came something sweet.
Judges 14:14

For three days the puzzled Philistines tried to solve the riddle,
but it continued to baffle them. Finally they asked Samson's bride
to find the answer. When she failed, they kept pressing her. At last
they resorted to blackmail, threatening to burn down her house
with her in it, if she did not give them the answer.

Frightened by their threats, Samson's bride wept during the
seven days of the feast. Unable to bear her tears any longer,
Samson revealed the answer, and she promptly told it to the
Philistines. At the banquet table on the last day of the feast, they
jubilantly answered the riddle,

What is sweeter than honey?
What is stronger than a lion?
Judges 14:18

Samson had lost his bet. Stung by the complicity of his bride
and his guests, he stormed into the city of Ashkelon, where he
killed thirty Philistines. To pay off his wager, he stripped their
bodies and brought back the spoils to the thirty men who had
answered his riddle.

THREE HUNDRED FOXES

Later when Samson went to Timnah to take his wife a present,
her father would not give him permission to see her, for he had
given her to another man. Again Samson turned his wrath against
the Philistines.

His feat of catching three hundred foxes is told in typical
folktale style. Binding the beasts together in pairs by their tails,

he fastened a burning torch to them. When he let these tortured, helpless creatures loose, they raced around madly, setting fire to the Philistines' fields of standing grain and to their olive trees. With their harvest destroyed, the Philistines avenged themselves on Samson's ex-wife and her father. The chain of violence continued, with Samson retaliating in a new slaughter of Philistines.

After this Samson had to hide in a mountain cave, but the Philistines knew how to get their man. They raided the tribe of Judah, letting it be known that it was really Samson they wanted. If he were turned over to them, they said they would let the men of Judah go in peace.

Seeing a large group of his countrymen approaching his hiding place to capture him, Samson did not resist, for he had no wish to hurt his own people. If they bound him and turned him over to the Philistines, he knew he was strong enough to break any shackles.

When he was delivered bound to the Philistines, they shouted and danced triumphantly. At last their hated enemy was safely in their power to do with as they chose, or so they thought. But "the Spirit of the Lord came mightily upon him, and the ropes which were on his arms became as flax that has caught fire, and his bonds melted off his hands" (Judg. 15:14).

Seizing the jawbone of an ass, Samson laid about him with his mighty strength, smiting the Philistines who had made sport of him. Finally, when his fury was spent, the field was covered with enemy dead.

Samson's mighty exertions had parched his mouth, so in his thirst he prayed to the Lord for water. Before him the earth opened and a spring appeared from which he drank and revived.

From that time on for twenty years, Samson became Israel's recognized leader against the Philistines. It seemed to his parents that all their hopes for their son were at last fulfilled.

STEALING THE GATES OF GAZA

Gaza, the chief city of the Philistines, was a formidable stronghold protected with thick walls and a heavy gate. In Gaza Samson became enamored of a harlot. Learning of this the Philistines lay in wait all night at the city gate to capture the Hebrew strong man when he should leave the woman's house. But Samson discovered their trap. At midnight "he arose and took hold of the doors of the gate of the city and the two posts, and pulled them up, bar and all, and put them on his shoulders and carried them to the top of the hill that is before Hebron" (Judg. 16:3).

SAMSON AND DELILAH

Samson's last romance was with Delilah, another Philistine woman. Amazed by the hero's great strength, the Philistines asked Delilah to find out his secret. Although she did her best to oblige her countrymen, Samson foiled three of her attempts. But her final trick he could not resist.

In a reproving fashion she asked, "How can you say, 'I love you,' when your heart is not with me? You have mocked me these three times, and you have not told me wherein your great strength lies" (Judg. 16:15).

Vexed by her continual wheedling, he told her his secret. From his birth he had been a Nazirite. No razor had ever touched his head, for if his seven locks were shorn, he would become weak like any other man.

That night while Samson slept, his head on Delilah's lap, a man came in and shaved Samson's head.

"The Philistines are upon you!" cried Delilah, waking him. Samson rubbed the sleep from his eyes and sprang to his feet. "I will go out as at other times, and shake myself free," declared the hero. But, as the story declares, "he did not know that the Lord had left him" (Judg. 16:20). He had betrayed his people and his mission. Bereft of his great strength, he became an easy prey to the Philistines.

EYELESS IN GAZA

His captors gouged out his eyes and bound him with bronze fetters to a millstone. Weak and helpless, he was forced to drive it ceaselessly around as a working slave.

News of him, blinded and bound in prison, must have broken his parents' hearts. To this ignominious state had their son of promise fallen through his own lust and the wiles of a woman.

Meanwhile, Samson felt his old strength returning as he ceaselessly turned the huge millstone, but no one noticed the change in him because he was a prisoner.

One day during a great feast held in honor of their national god, Dagon, the Philistines decided that they wanted to see Samson. It would be great sport to enjoy the humiliation of the former strong man who had been Israel's mighty hero. Hundreds of people crowded into the temple for the spectacle; even the roof was packed with onlookers.

A subdued and docile Samson was sent for and placed between the temple's great stone pillars for all to see. Then Samson bent down to whisper to the young lad who led him by the hand, "Let me feel the pillars on which the house rests, that I may lean against them" (Judg. 16:26).

Samson stretched out his huge arms, blindly groping for the two middle pillars of the temple. As he flexed his great muscles, he knew his superhuman strength had revived. In one final orgy of destruction he summoned the last ounce of his immense power and pushed against the pillars until they buckled and broke, causing the walls to collapse in a great cloud of broken stone. Underneath lay hundreds of Philistines and the blind hero of Israel, buried in the ruins of Dagon's temple.

MEANING OF SAMSON'S STORY

The serious reader who expects to find stories of deep religious significance in the Bible is surprised to encounter such crude and exaggerated tales as those of Samson. Here are folk tales somewhat reminiscent of the American Paul Bunyan stories. Samson is one of those strong but foolish heroes who so often fall short of their goals. Why was his story included in the Bible?

The Scriptures were written for all people. Some respond to the strong personalities of Moses and Joshua; others find valuable lessons in the heroic yet human image of Samson. The story of his life abundantly shows that God can use many different kinds of people to carry out His purpose.

Samson was a man of contradictions. He was a son of promise, yet he caused unending disappointment to his people and especially his pious but overindulgent parents. Endowed with tremendous strength, he often used it in senseless violence. As Israel's champion against the Philistines, he was repeatedly victimized by Philistine women. Brought up as a dedicated Nazirite, he was continually defeated by his own uncontrolled appetites. Through his death he accomplished his greatest defeat of the enemy and fulfilled the destiny for which he was set apart at birth. Such was the strong yet stupid man, the folk hero Samson.

V

R U T H

THE FOREIGNER

PROLOGUE

From tales of cruel carnage in the Book of Judges, we turn to the serenely beautiful story of Ruth. It is an idyll set in the period of the judges, yet seems untouched by the violent history of that time. A young Moabite woman named Ruth is the heroine of this novel whose theme is God's inclusive love for all men.

The story opens in Judah, where the rains had failed. To escape this drought which had caused crops to wither in the fields and famine to stalk Judean villages, Elimelech, with his wife Naomi and his two sons, decided to leave their home in Bethlehem. After packing up their belongings, they journeyed eastward, beyond the Jordan and the Dead Sea, into the land of Moab, home of Israel's inveterate enemies. Yet here the family from Bethlehem found food, just as the sons of Jacob had long before found grain in Egypt during a drought.

Soon Elimelech died, leaving Naomi to bring up her sons in a strange land. Moab proved to be a friendly place, where the two young men, Mahlon and Chilion, fell in love with Moabite women and married them.

The names of the characters indicate the story's symbolic nature, for Naomi means "sweet" or "pleasant," while Mahlon means "sickness" and Chilion "wasting" or "consumption." Their Moabite wives were Orpah and Ruth, the first probably meaning "turn back," the second, "companion" or "friend." The names epitomize the fate or personality of the actors in the drama.

FAREWELLS IN MOAB

After ten years of happiness, both of Naomi's sons died in Moab, leaving her an old woman with no sons or grandsons to carry on the family. No worse fate could befall a Hebrew woman. To her, it must have seemed an act of God's judgment. Sadly she prepared to leave the land which had sheltered her family. Rumors had reached her that crops were again flourishing in Bethlehem and there she now longed to spend her declining years.

Naomi's two daughters-in-law set out with her on the homeward journey, but in her loving concern for them, she urged them to remain in Moab and return to their parents' homes. Why should Orpah and Ruth, who were still young women, bind themselves to the hopeless future of an old widow bereft of her sons?

While the three women wept again, Orpah kissed her mother-in-law but, true to her name, she turned back to her family, her country, and her gods.

Ruth, however, clung to Naomi, uttering the unforgettable words, "Entreat me not to leave you or to return from following you; for where you go I will go, and where you lodge I will lodge; your people shall be my people, and your God my God; where you die I will die, and there will I be buried. May the Lord do so to me and more also if even death parts me from you" (Ruth 1:16-17).

Though originally a young woman's declaration of loyalty to her mother-in-law, this familiar passage has become a favorite one for weddings, expressing as it does the quality of belonging that should be part of the marriage bond.

BACK TO BETHLEHEM

Naomi's old friends in Bethlehem turned out to greet her on her arrival. Though sorrows had aged her, people knew her well enough to address her by name. "Do not call me Naomi," she cried, for sweetness and pleasantness had left her. "Call me Mara [meaning "bitter"], for the Almighty has dealt very bitterly with me. I went away full, and the Lord has brought me back empty. Why call me Naomi, when the Lord has afflicted me and the Almighty has brought calamity upon me?" (Ruth 1:20-21).

Despite her sorrows, Naomi was wise enough to know that life must go on. The dead cannot be called back to life. Ruth, too, was not one to despair, but accepted the situation for what it was. Both women now faced the pressing problem of finding a livelihood for themselves.

Ruth and Naomi reached Bethlehem when harvesters were beginning to reap the barley. Having no crop of their own, the women could only exercise the old right of the poor, guaranteed them by law, to glean in the fields of more fortunate neighbors.

The law stated, "When you reap the harvest of your land, you shall not reap your field to its very border, neither shall you gather the gleanings after your harvest. And you shall not strip your vineyard bare, neither shall you gather the fallen grapes of your vineyard; you shall leave them for the poor and for the sojourner: I am the Lord your God" (Lev. 19:9-10).

RUTH THE GLEANER

Ruth followed the harvesters as they reaped ripe grain and bound it into sheaves. She patiently gathered up loose stalks in a field belonging to Boaz, a remote kinsman of her father-in-law Elimelech.

A happy patriarchal relationship existed between Boaz and his reapers, for he was no taskmaster but the sort of farmer who respected the work of those who helped him. As master and servants belonged to the same cultural and religious community, Boaz did not consider himself above his workers. Nobody dominated and everyone was pleasantly happy.

Seeing the fair young stranger in his fields, Boaz asked, "Whose maiden is this?" (Ruth 2:5).

His overseer replied, "It is the Moabite maiden, who came back with Naomi from the country of Moab" (Ruth 2:6). After asking his permission to glean, she had worked hard since early morning.

Boaz himself approached Ruth, urging her not to wander off to other fields, but to continue gleaning among his maidens. He assured her that his young men had been instructed not to annoy her. As a final sign of his welcome he invited her, when thirsty, to drink water from the vessels provided for his workers.

Thanking her benefactor in a typically oriental manner, Ruth uttered the key word of the tale. "Why have I found favor in your eyes, that you should take notice of me, when I am a foreigner?" (Ruth 2:10).

People in Bethlehem had already noted and talked approvingly about Ruth's loving consideration for her mother-in-law, so that Boaz and his neighbors felt very kindly disposed toward her. They approved of her family loyalty. Everyone applauded her courageous determination to earn a living for herself and the older woman.

"The Lord recompense you for what you have done," exclaimed Boaz, "and a full reward be given you by the Lord, the God of Israel, under whose wings you have come to take refuge!" (Ruth 2:12).

At mealtime Boaz invited her to eat with his reapers. After all were satisfied, a little food remained. Remembering the empty larder at home, Ruth set this food aside for Naomi.

In the afternoon Boaz did more than the law required. He told his servants to leave extra grain for Ruth and to let her glean among the sheaves. As a result of his generosity, she carried home nearly a bushel measure, an ephah of barley, together with the food she had saved for her mother-in-law.

"Where did you glean today?" Naomi asked the tired but happy young woman.

When Naomi learned that Ruth had worked in the field of Boaz, the older woman advised her daughter-in-law to remain there until the end of the harvest so that she would not be molested.

NAOMI'S MATCHMAKING

It was Naomi's shrewd suggestion that Ruth follow up her favorable beginnings with Boaz. These might well develop into a deeper relationship. Should they lead to a husband and family for Ruth, so much the better. Naomi could then look forward not only to a secure old age but to her heart's desire—grandchildren to bring joy to her declining years.

Naomi knew that the barley would be winnowed in the steady afternoon wind that blows until sunset. Afterward Boaz would surely stay at his threshing floor to guard the grain during the dark hours of night. The situation was one to be utilized—all within the limits of decorum and the accepted morality of the time. As Boaz did not seem to realize that a beautiful young woman was waiting for him, Naomi determined to awaken him to that fact.

"Wash therefore and anoint yourself, and put on your best clothes and go down to the threshing floor," Naomi instructed Ruth. "But do not make yourself known to the man until he has finished eating and drinking. But when he lies down, observe the place where he lies; then, go and uncover his feet and lie down; and he will tell you what to do" (Ruth 3:3-4).

The plan worked. At midnight when Boaz turned and saw a woman, he asked in surprise, "Who are you?"

She replied, "I am Ruth, your maidservant" (Ruth 3:9). Then she said, "You are next of kin," intimating that Boaz had a family obligation to her. Naomi must have coached her well, for Ruth was already familiar with Israel's law. Hebrew law permitted a childless widow to marry her deceased husband's brother or other near relative in order to assure the continuation of her husband's family.

BOAZ AND RUTH

Boaz willingly acknowledged his obligation as one of the next of kin. He was both surprised and pleased that Ruth had approached him rather than one of the younger men who already admired her for her virtue and value.

"May you be blessed by the Lord, my daughter," he said; "you have made this last kindness greater than the first, in that you have not gone after young men, whether poor or rich. And now, my daughter, do not fear, I will do for you all that you ask, for all my fellow townsmen know that you are a woman of worth" (Ruth 3:10-11).

His quick, enthusiastic response indicates that Boaz had already been turning over in his mind the possibilities Ruth presented to him. He knew, however, that one obstacle stood in the way of his fulfilling his pleasant duty—there was a nearer kinsman than himself who, according to law, would have a prior claim to Ruth. With a promise that he would arrange the matter for her, Boaz gave her six measures of barley for her mother-in-law.

Naomi smiled a pleased smile to herself as she saw Ruth returning with a lavish present of grain. The plan was succeeding, as the older woman knew it would. From her store of worldly wisdom, Naomi advised Ruth, "Wait, my daughter, until you learn how the matter turns out, for the man will not rest, but will settle the matter today" (Ruth 3:18).

LEGAL BUSINESS AT THE CITY GATE

At the city gate, where the men usually assembled to discuss public affairs, Boaz gathered ten elders of the city. Among the Jews, ten is still the minimum number, the *minyan* or quorum required for such acts as establishing a synagogue or giving the marriage benediction. There is general agreement that Ruth 4:2 is the first evidence for the rule that ten men constitute a quorum.

In the presence of the ten elders, Boaz challenged the other kinsman to buy from Naomi the plot of land once belonging to her husband. As she must now have been almost destitute, it was a relative's duty to redeem her land so as to keep it in the family. At first the man agreed to an outright sale, but when Boaz mentioned Ruth and the obligations of the levirate, the kinsman changed his mind and renounced his right to the land, saying, "I cannot redeem it for myself, lest I mar mine own inheritance" (Ruth 4:6).

What did he mean? It is believed that according to Hebrew law, if the kinsman had purchased the land he would have been obliged to marry Ruth. Their son would have been considered the son of Ruth's first husband, and the field would have reverted to him as the true heir. Such an outcome would have endangered the kinsman's bequests to his own heirs. He could not afford to exercise his rights.

To signify his decision, the kinsman pulled off his sandal and gave it to Boaz who stepped into the other shoe. We use the expression today when one man takes over another's place.

HAPPY ENDING

Boaz was now free both to buy Naomi's field and to marry the foreign woman, Ruth. The elders at the gate confirmed the legality of these actions by witnessing them. In an atmosphere of rejoicing, the ten men added their blessing, mentioning not only the patriarchal mothers Rachel and Leah, but Tamar, who had long before invoked the levirate law of marriage (Gen. 38).

Naomi lived to see the impossible happen. Once she had believed she would never again hold a baby belonging to her own family, but now in her old arms she cradled the infant son of Ruth and Boaz.

Naomi's neighbors rejoiced with her and said, "Blessed be the Lord, who has not left you this day without next of kin; and may his name be renowned in Israel! He shall be to you a restorer of life and a nourisher of your old age; for your daughter-in-law who loves you, who is more to you than seven sons, has borne him" (Ruth 4:14-15).

Saving the climax for his very last word, the storyteller brings his tale to its astonishing conclusion. "And the women of the neighborhood gave him a name, saying, 'A son has been born to Naomi.' They named him Obed; he was the father of Jesse, the father of David" (Ruth 4:17).

MEANING OF RUTH'S STORY

Thus in the person of Israel's greatest and most beloved king, the dark question overhanging Ruth's story is triumphantly answered. A foreigner, daughter of the hated Moabites, became a great-grandmother of David, Israel's most illustrious ruler.

Though by reason of her race Ruth was under legal indictment, "No . . . Moabite shall enter the assembly of the Lord; even to the tenth generation" (Deut. 23:3), her human qualities prevailed. The story does not mention any ritual conversion. Ruth simply chose Naomi's God, "your God shall be my God," and placed herself under His protection. Her exemplary character won for her the approval of her Bethlehem neighbors.

The Hebrew people placed great emphasis on their conviction that they were God's Chosen People. God's choice, the Scriptures show, was not on the basis of any outstanding merit on the people's part, but was solely a matter of His election. Nevertheless, Israel was a special people among the sea of diverse groups inhabiting the earth.

On the other hand, the Hebrews slowly came to a realization that God is the Father of all peoples. Because He is their Creator, all races, tribes, and nations belong to the brotherhood of mankind.

Tension between these two ideas—that of the Chosen People and that of God's inclusive love for all men—emerges again and again in Hebrew history. Sometimes the latter idea was eloquently expressed, but more often the former was dominant. Joshua tried to exterminate foreigners from the Holy Land, but when this proved impossible, the Hebrews learned to live with those who had inhabited the country before them.

Samson, the strong man, was not thrust out of his tribe for marrying a non-Hebrew, despite his parents' disapproval of the marriage.

In later Hebrew history, when the Jews were released from their Babylonian captivity, a wave of exclusiveness swept Israel. According to Nehemiah 13, all Hebrew husbands married to women of foreign descent were required to divorce these wives, in an effort to establish a pure-blooded Hebrew nation.

The Book of Ruth was written to counteract such isolationism. Its story of a foreigner from a hostile country quietly entering the community of Israel in which she became an honored member of the once-exclusive group, bore witness to the brotherhood of all mankind. Ruth's story dramatized Israel's belief that the promise and blessing Abraham received were not confined to a limited family, but were given to all people in the family of man.

Bethlehem became the ancestral town of Israel's royal family, for here the young woman from Moab had borne her son. And it was in this same town, the city of David, that, centuries later, Mary bore Jesus, the Messiah whose mission was to all men.

Ruth's story foreshadows the inclusiveness of Christianity, which reaches out to embrace all peoples. Peter, the Jew, expressed this aspect of Christianity when he said to the pagan Roman centurion who wanted to become a member of the Christian community, "Truly I perceive that God shows no partiality, but in every nation any one who fears him and does what is right is acceptable to him" (Acts 10:34-35).

VI

SAMUEL
THE KINGMAKER

FAMILY BACKGROUND

In the rugged hill country of Ephraim, which stretched across the central mountain range of Palestine, lived a well-to-do Hebrew named Elkanah. Both his name, meaning "God owns" or "God possesses," and his story indicate that he was among the pious men of Israel. Each year Elkanah took his family on a pilgrimage to the sanctuary at Shiloh, at that time the center of Israel's religious life. Here the old priest Eli and his two sons guarded Israel's shrine, the sacred Ark of the Covenant. It was a chest of acacia wood overlaid with gold and decorated with golden cherubim, but all Israel believed it to be the dwelling-place of the Lord of hosts.

Here for the first time, the Scriptures ascribe to God the title Lord of Hosts, or as the older translations render it, Lord of Sabaoth (I Sam. 1:3). "Hosts" refers to the armies of Israel, a meaning made clear in David's claim, "I come to you in the name of the Lord of Hosts, the God of the armies of Israel" (I Sam. 17:45). The new title indicates a shift in Israel's understanding of Yahweh. "Lord of hosts" is the cry of a downtrodden people for divine leadership in battle. With God at the head of their armies they believed total victory possible.

Elkanah's entire family went along on the annual excursions to Shiloh. At the sanctuary, they would all share in the generous sacrifice he had provided.

But Elkanah was troubled.

One worry was personal and concerned his wife Hannah. Children were to him and to his contemporaries a special blessing in that they ensured the continuation of a man's life. It was considered a curse to be childless. Hannah was childless, a circumstance that brought grief to them both. Her name meant "gracious is Yahweh," but at this time her barrenness made her name seem incongruous. As was frequently done in those days, Elkanah had married a second wife, Peninnah, meaning "pearl" or "red coral," who bore him sons and daughters to keep his name alive in Ephraim.

PHILISTINE DOMINATION

Elkanah also worried about the troubled political situation of his day. He lived at the close of the period of the "judges" when Philistine domination hung over the confederation of Hebrew tribes. Samson of the tribe of Dan had been one leader engaged in armed conflict with this enemy. He had fought them, but had not permanently conquered them.

These Philistines, "peoples of the sea" as the Pharaoh Ramses III called them when they first appeared about 1200 B.C., are of unknown origin. Before their attempted invasion of Egypt, they had been in Crete and other islands of the Aegean world between Asia Minor and Greece. From the Hittites, whose power in northern Syria the Philistines helped to break, these warlike people learned the secret of making iron weapons. But the Philistines, no match for the Egyptians, were beaten back when they attempted to invade Egypt. Their defeat is pictured on the walls of Ramses III's temple at Medinet Habu in Egypt.

In these wall decorations the Philistines appear quite different from the Hebrews or other Semitic peoples. They were tall and their warriors wore distinctive feathered helmets which increased their apparent size. Their features were those usually associated with the Greeks.

Egypt was only too glad to see these fierce fighters settle beyond her borders, along the coast of southwestern Palestine. The entire region of Palestine, as we have already noted, took its name from this migrating Aegean people, but the area they actually controlled was confined to the coastal plain in the vicinity of the five great Philistine cities of Gaza, Gath, Ashkelon, Ashdod, and Ekron. From these, with their efficient military organization, the Philistines threatened the Hebrew tribes living in the central part of the country.

Because Palestine's southern harbors were controlled by the Philistines and her northern ones by the Phoenicians, the Hebrews had no access to the sea and never developed an affinity for it. Major seafaring is not a part of Jewish classical history.

Elkanah was as troubled as other Israelites about the Philistine danger. Were his children growing up in a world in which they would always be the underdog? Enemy garrisons were strategically located to keep the Hebrews in their place. The craft of iron smelting, a well-kept secret of the Philistines, gave them superior weapons. Smiths were not allowed in Hebrew territory. When a tribesman needed to sharpen his farming tools he must take them down to smiths in the coastal country. "Now there was no smith to be found throughout all the land of Israel; for the Philistines said, 'Lest the Hebrews make themselves swords or spears'; but every one of the Israelites went down to the Philistines to sharpen his plowshare, his mattock, his axe, or his sickle" (I Sam. 13:19-20).

Throughout Israel there was discontent, for the Hebrews knew they were far behind their neighbors in might and prosperity.

Had Yahweh forgotten His people? Was He indeed the victorious God of their fathers? Elkanah knew that, unlike many of his fellow tribesmen, he would always remain loyal to the faith of his fathers. But in the face of Hebrew weakness and disunity could his faith survive as a vital force in the lives of his children? If only someone like Moses or Joshua would arise to lead the tribes in the name of the Lord God of Israel, he might have mused, little dreaming that he was to be the father of such a leader.

HANNAH AT SHILOH

One year Hannah was so unhappy at Shiloh that her mood overshadowed the family's usual enjoyment of the feast. As a good husband and provider, Elkanah had given each of his wives their offerings, but of course Peninnah received extra ones for her children. Thus at the very altar before the Ark, the shameful difference between Elkanah's two wives became apparent. In this situation Peninnah was no comfort, for she taunted her rival and made the most of her preferred position as a mother. Peninnah's mockery caused Hannah to weep and refuse to eat.

Seeing his wife's tears, Elkanah gently asked, "Hannah, why do you weep? And why do you not eat? And why is your heart sad? Am I not more to you than ten sons?" (I Sam. 1:8).

But Hannah knew that their deep love for each other could never be a substitute for the son she longed for. As soon as the festival meal was over, she went to the shrine, for she wanted to be alone to pour out her grief before her God and pray again for a son.

"She was deeply distressed and prayed to the Lord, and wept bitterly. And she vowed a vow and said, 'O Lord of hosts, if thou wilt indeed look on the affliction of thy maidservant . . . but wilt give to thy maidservant a son, then I will give him to the Lord all the days of his life, and no razor shall touch his head' "

(I Sam. 1:10-11). Thus she promised to make the son for whom she prayed a Nazirite, as Samson had been, vowed from his birth to the service of God.

When Eli, the priest of the sanctuary, saw Hannah standing there mumbling to herself, he thought the festival wine had gone to her head as it apparently often did with other worshipers. When he accused Hannah of being a drunken woman, she told him her story and he sent her away encouraged by his blessing. "Go in peace, and the God of Israel grant your petition which you have made to him" (I Sam. 1:17).

The next year, as the son for whom she had prayed had just been born, Hannah did not accompany her family on their annual pilgrimage. She wanted to keep her baby with her until he was weaned and ready to enter the service of God at Shiloh, as she had promised. Thus Samuel, like many of the Bible's great personalities, was marked as special from his birth.

Hannah called her young son Samuel, which means "name of God." Strangely enough the Bible indicates that his name means "I have asked him of the Lord" (I Sam. 1:20), but this is actually the correct translation of Saul's name. How or when this puzzling change occurred we do not know.

HANNAH'S SONG

A beautiful psalm is ascribed to Hannah on the occasion when she presented her son to the Lord. This song of praise is strikingly similar to the one Mary sang when she knew she was to be the mother of Jesus. Apparently this later hymn, often called the Magnificat from its opening word in the Latin version, was modeled on Hannah's, for both contain lines that correspond to each other. Hannah sang,

> The Lord makes poor and makes rich;
> he brings low, he also exalts.

He raises up the poor from the dust;
  He lifts the needy from the ash heap,
to make them sit with princes
  and inherit a seat of honor.

I Sam. 2:7-8

In the same vein, Mary sang,

He has put down the mighty from their thrones,
and exalted those of low degree;
he has filled the hungry with good things,
and the rich he has sent empty away.

Luke 1:52-53

Social problems, with their requirements of justice and compassion, occupy an important place in the writings of the great eighth-century prophets, but even in Hannah's time in the eleventh century, many of these problems had been recognized and dealt with in Israel's laws. It is not surprising that in Hannah's day God was conceived of as One who does not measure the value of a human being by his wealth or honors. Before God, all men are equal. The Hebrews knew that worldly judgments are often wrong and that "not by might shall a man prevail" (I Sam. 2:9). The day would come when God, appearing as a Judge, would institute a society founded on true values and ruled by justice. Hannah's song can be interpreted as a proclamation of these truths. It is fitting that Samuel's mother expressed a faith in which personal salvation and a satisfying contact with God are not the only elements. For her son, active efforts to better man's social and political condition became a cornerstone of faith.

YOUNG SAMUEL MINISTERS IN THE SANCTUARY

It may have been hard at first for the boy Samuel to leave his mother and a family in which he was the favored youngest child, but he soon slipped into the routine of ministering in the Lord's sanctuary at Shiloh. There, clad in a linen ephod, the apron-like garment priests wore as a symbol of their holy office, the boy went about his duties, guarding the Ark, cleaning and replenishing the lamp that burned before it, and performing other tasks under the supervision of Eli, the old priest in charge of the temple. His parents had apprenticed him to Eli so that he might learn all that a priest should know. When his family came to Shiloh on their annual pilgrimage, his mother brought him a robe she had made for him. Each year the garment was larger than the last, for he grew fast (I Sam. 2:19).

While young Samuel learned to serve the Lord, Eli's two priest sons, Hophni and Phineas, brought disgrace upon their calling. The Bible describes them as "worthless men; they had no regard for the Lord" (I Sam. 2:12). As some priests of every religion in all ages have done, they used religion for their own enrichment. Even worse, "they lay with the women who served at the entrance to the tent of meeting" (I Sam. 2:22), imitating the idolatrous practices of the Canaanites. Because of the priests' misuse of their holy office, "the word of the Lord was rare in those days; there was no frequent vision" (I Sam. 3:1).

"SPEAK, LORD, FOR THY SERVANT HEARS"

One night while the lamp before the Ark still burned in the temple where young Samuel slept, a voice calling his name awakened him. Three times he heard the words, "Samuel! Samuel!" and three times he hastened to Eli only to be told that the old priest had not called. After the third time, Eli, realizing that it was the Lord, instructed Samuel to reply, "Speak, Lord, for thy servant hears" (I Sam. 3:9).

When the voice called again, Samuel answered as he had been taught and received the announcement of God's judgment on Eli's family. "I am about to punish his house for ever, for the iniquity which he knew, because his sons were blaspheming God, and he did not restrain them" (I Sam. 3:13).

In the morning Samuel hesitated to deliver his message of doom, but pressed by the old priest, the youth spared him nothing. Eli, an old man despairing over his delinquent sons, resigned himself to the Lord's will, awaiting the inevitable day when punishment would fall on his house.

As Samuel grew toward manhood, it became known that the Lord was with him. Men came to him to learn God's will, and he became a prophet in Israel. "And all Israel from Dan to Beersheba knew that Samuel was established as a prophet of the Lord. And the Lord appeared again at Shiloh, for the Lord revealed himself to Samuel" (I Sam. 3:20-21).

MILITARY DISASTERS

Before Israel advanced to a new phase of her history, the tribes faced a period of military defeat at the hands of the Philistines. Men often seem to need competition with an opponent or even a hostile enemy to develop the best or the worst in themselves. The Egyptian opposition and the difficulties during the Exodus under Moses gave Israel its faith. The struggle against the Canaanites during the settlement of the Promised Land under Joshua gave Israel its national home. Under the leadership of Samuel, the wars with the Philistines gave Israel its kings and its national reawakening.

In a desperate attempt to check the enemy's advance into the central highlands, the Israelites established their camp of war at Ebenezer in the fertile lowlands of central Canaan. Not far away, at Aphek, where the Philistine warriors gathered, their chariots were drawn up ready for battle. When the first clash occurred, the Israelites bravely stood their ground against the dreaded chariots, but were finally forced to retire leaving many dead upon the battlefield.

While sitting dejectedly in their camp listening to the victorious Philistines shouting across the valley, the Israelites pondered the meaning of their defeat. Why had the Lord failed them? Why had He permitted the enemy to inflict such a humiliating defeat upon them?

As a last desperate expedient, someone proposed, "Let us bring the ark of the covenant of the Lord here from Shiloh, that he may come among us and save us from the power of our enemies" (I Sam. 4:3).

Wild shouts greeted this plan to bring God Himself into the battle on their behalf. In their way, the Israelites of Samuel's day tried to do what Aaron had attempted long ago—they endeavored to capture God in a visible form and force Him to do something for them. But the God of Israel is not like the idols of other peoples. He is not an image to be carried on the shoulders of priests. It is idolatrous to use Yahweh as a good luck charm or a substitute for a man's own effort and moral strength. No man can force God to do anything, for it is God, not man, who makes the decisions.

Brought from Shiloh on the shoulders of Hophni and Phinehas, the Ark arrived in the Hebrew camp to the sound of tumultuous rejoicing. So loud were the shouts of the Israelite warriors that the very earth seemed to resound with them (I Sam. 4:5).

The shouting across the valley frightened the Philistines, who exclaimed in alarm, "A god has come into the camp" (I Sam. 4:7). In saying "a god" rather than "*the* God," they were merely interpreting the thoughts of the Israelites themselves who, on this occasion, were treating Yahweh as one of many gods.

Goaded by fear of this unknown God, the Philistines hurled their forces against Israel in a desperate attack. Everywhere on the battlefield they were victorious.

BAD NEWS FOR ELI

All day at Shiloh, the old priest Eli trembled, growing faint at heart as he awaited news of the battle. Anxiously he wondered how his sons fared in the midst of the fighting and how Israel was defending her most sacred object, the Ark of the Covenant.

Soon a panting messenger arrived with horror in his eyes. His torn clothes and the earth sprinkled on his head, both signs of mourning, proclaimed his message before he spoke. With mounting despair Eli listened to his catalogue of defeat.

"Israel has fled before the Philistines, and there has also been a great slaughter among the people; your two sons also, Hophni and Phinehas, are dead, and the ark of God has been captured" (I Sam. 4:17).

At the messenger's last words, Eli fell over backward from his seat, broke his neck, and died. The Bible simply comments that he was an old man and heavy.

All was over for Israel. Even their main sanctuary at Shiloh disappeared from history at this point. What sort of catastrophe struck the place we do not know, but archaeological diggings at the site reveal that the city was completely razed. Later on Jeremiah used the name of Shiloh as an example of total destruction (Jer. 7:14). But the silence of the Book of Samuel about the fate of this sanctuary is more impressive than the worst report of destruction could be.

From every point of view—military, political, religious—Israel suffered complete defeat. What future lay ahead for Samuel, the prophet, now that the Ark he had guarded since childhood was lost, Eli dead, and Shiloh itself destroyed? Surely the bright promise of his youth was in danger of being extinguished in the general ruin of the Chosen People.

THE CAPTURED ARK

The Philistines were too much in awe of the Ark, impotent though it had been in battle, to destroy the sacred object. First they installed it as a trophy in the sanctuary of their god, Dagon, at Ashdod. However, the next morning they were shocked to find Dagon's image fallen on its face from the pedestal. When this happened again and the head and hands of Dagon's image were broken off, the people of Ashdod could not get rid of the Ark soon enough. It was taken to Gath, but when bubonic plague broke out in that city, it was sent on to Ekron. Plague appeared there also. After seven months the Philistines had had enough of the Ark. It had become a curse rather than a blessing.

Deeply puzzled, the Philistines could not understand why Israel's God did not help them now that they possessed His holy dwelling. It was beyond their comprehension that Yahweh did not dwell in a box made by human hands, nor act at man's command. To rid themselves of the curse that seemed to follow the Ark, they returned it to the Israelites with strange guilt offerings. They reproduced in gold the tumors and the mice that plagued them and brought these objects as an acknowledgment of their guilt. Thus they transformed what they believed to be their guilt and its punishment into a visible object. It was a kind of visual confessional.

Using one of their oxcarts, they dragged the Ark to the border at Beth-shemesh, the field of Joshua. When some curious Israelites ventured to look inside the sacred chest, they were immediately punished by the Divine Presence. Did they expect to see an idol like those of the Philistines or Canaanites? It is amazing how little the Israelites knew about their own faith. Only a small minority of them really understood its essentials and lived according to its requirements.

Because the ancient sanctuary of Shiloh, the center of Israel's worship, lay in ruins, the Ark was carried on to Kiriath-jearim to the hilltop home of a certain man named Abinadab. There, in the custody of his son Eleazar, a priest, the sacred chest remained for some years.

SAMUEL RESTORES ISRAEL

Samuel did not mourn long for the vanished sanctuary of his youth. The Lord still spoke to him and there was work for him to do. He turned all his energy to the spiritual restoration of Israel. If the people were to triumph over their foes he knew they must cast out all heathen idols.

"If you are returning to the Lord with all your heart," he exhorted them, "then put away the foreign gods and the Ashtaroth from among you, and direct your heart to the Lord, and serve him only, and he will deliver you out of the hand of the Philistines" (I Sam. 7:3).

The people listened to Samuel and made him their judge, bringing to him all kinds of difficult problems. He established headquarters at Ramah, his old home town, where he built an altar to the Lord, but every year he traveled to other sanctuaries, Bethel, Gilgal, and Mizpah, administering justice and defending the weak and helpless.

At Mizpah, the Israelites routed an attacking force of their old enemy, "so the Philistines were subdued and did not again enter the territory of Israel" (I Sam. 7:13). For a time there was peace in the land.

Samuel, the great judge and prophet leader, working for the rebuilding of Israel as the people of God, could not face a bitter truth: God's kingship over the federation of tribes was not working out. Israel lacked the necessary faith, the wholehearted religious commitment, to make God's sovereignty succeed within the historical framework of the ancient world.

Today it is often said that religion has declined from the days of our ancestors and has become external and showy, expressing itself only in numbers and not in quality or depth. Has this not always been true? Here in the time of Samuel we see Israel so weak and imperfect that the kingship of God over the tribes failed.

The attempt to rule Israel by dynasties of priests had also failed. Eli and his two corrupt sons had been swept away. Even Samuel's sons proved unworthy of their great father, for they "did not walk in his ways, but turned aside after gain; they took bribes and perverted justice" (I Sam. 8:3). Samuel was blind to his sons' misconduct and the failure of his dream of God as Ruler over the Chosen People. How was Israel to be saved in this crisis?

"GIVE US A KING!"

The elders of Israel found the answer. They came to Samuel with their request, "Give us a king to govern us" (I Sam. 8:6).

Samuel was displeased by their demand, but God, knowing the nature of His people, opened the prophet's mind. "Hearken to the voice of the people in all that they say to you; for they have not rejected you, but they have rejected me from being king over them" (I Sam. 8:7).

Since the days of their ancestors in the wilderness, the Chosen People had often turned from the Lord. Yet God did not deny their request for a king. God's patience with man is perhaps the most amazing feature in the Scriptures.

Samuel, having observed the practices in royal households, warned his people of the evils of strong central power in the hands of an absolute king. Priest-judge that he was, he was as much concerned with Israel's social welfare as with her spiritual life.

These will be the ways of the king who will reign over you: he will
take your sons and appoint them to his chariots and to be his horsemen,
and to run before his chariots; and he will appoint for himself commanders of thousands and commanders of fifties, and some to plow
his ground and to reap his harvest, and to make his implements of war
and the equipment of his chariots. He will take your daughters to be
perfumers and cooks and bakers. He will take the best of your fields
and vineyards and olive orchards and give them to his servants. He
will take the tenth of your grain and of your vineyards and give it to
his officers and to his servants. He will take your menservants and
maidservants, and the best of your cattle and your asses, and put them
to his work. He will take the tenth of your flocks, and you shall be
his slaves.   I Sam. 8:11-17

Israel was tired of being a second-class power. Only a king,
they thought, could give them equal status with other nations.
"No!" they shouted to all Samuel's advice, "but we will have a
king over us, that we also may be like all the nations, and that
our king may govern us and go out before us and fight our
battles" (I Sam. 8:19-20).

The die was cast. Israel was willing to give up its special
character as the Chosen People of the Lord in order to be like
other nations. The desire to conform, to be like everybody else,
usually a manifestation of youth, is here displayed by an entire
nation.

"SERVE HIM FAITHFULLY WITH ALL YOUR HEART"

Ironically it was Samuel, the man most opposed to a monarchy,
who was charged with finding Israel a king. When he anointed
Saul to the kingship, the old prophet brought to an end the long
period of Israel's judges, of whom he was the last. The tribal
confederation now became a kingdom.

Samuel was a man standing on the threshold of a new order.
Behind him lay troubled years of political transition through

which he had served his people well, and they honored him for it. His life had not been happy, weighed down as he was by the disappointment of worthless sons, his continual anxiety for Israel, and, in his later years, the failure of Saul's reign. Yet he never ceased to intercede for his people.

Since his childhood days at Shiloh he had held fast to the ancient faith in Yahweh. This was the faith he commended to his people in his farewell.

"Only fear the Lord, and serve him faithfully with all your heart; for consider what great things he has done for you" (I Sam. 12:24).

VII

SAUL
THE TRAGIC KING

SEARCH FOR LOST DONKEYS

Saul comes striding into history on a lowly mission. His father Kish, a prosperous farmer of the tribe of Benjamin, had sent him out with a servant to find some lost donkeys. Saul looked everywhere, straining his eyes to scan rocky upland pastures where the animals might have strayed. At his side his servant must have struggled to keep up with his master's long steps, for Saul was far taller than most men.

The Scriptures describe him in admiring words. "There was not a man among the people of Israel more handsome than he; from his shoulders upward he was taller than any of the people" (I Sam. 9:2). Moreover, his personality was so attractive that all his life he was able to charm his countrymen, to inspire them to great efforts under his leadership. He seemed to take his exceptional qualities for granted, not realizing that his instant success with others came to him as a gift and that many people have to struggle to win similar success.

After three days of fruitless search, the food in their sacks was almost gone, so Saul decided to turn homeward. It was better to arrive empty-handed than to cause his father anxiety for their safety.

75

But when they came in sight of the city of Ramathaim-zophim, the servant suggested that they enter it to consult Samuel, the famous man of God who lived there. "He is a man that is held in honor," explained the servant; "all that he says comes true. Let us go there; perhaps he can tell us about the journey on which we have set out" (I Sam. 9:6).

Saul hesitated, but when the servant produced a fourth of a shekel of silver to pay the seer, the two men turned toward Samuel's home.

At this point in the story, some ancient editor inserted a sentence to explain to readers of his day the meaning of the word "seer." "Formerly in Israel, when a man went to inquire of God, he said, 'Come, let us go to the seer'; for he who is now called a prophet was formerly called a seer" (I Sam. 9:9). This insertion shows that even Hebrew readers of an early period found some of the older texts of the Bible difficult to understand.

If explanations and interpretations were useful thousands of years ago, how much more necessary are they today? We approach these old stories with reverence and also with a desire to learn their truth. Though we shall not find answers to all our questions about the ancient writings through careful modern study and research, these methods will help us see more clearly the essential teachings of the Bible.

SAUL MEETS SAMUEL

When Saul reached the city gate, he enquired of a man coming toward him, "Tell me where is the house of the seer?" (I Sam. 9:18).

"I am the seer," replied the man, for he was no other than the great prophet himself.

Samuel searched the face of the tall young stranger standing before him. The prophet was not surprised by Saul's abrupt arrival, for the Lord had said that at this very hour He would send him a man from the tribe of Benjamin who was to be anointed prince over the people. In Samuel's eyes this handsome young man of commanding presence and regal bearing was worthy of being a king.

For the moment, however, the old prophet kept his own counsel, merely inviting Saul to share a festival meal with him at the high place of worship. Almost casually Samuel told Saul that his lost donkeys had been found.

The high place to which Samuel led Saul was a hilltop sanctuary, for the Hebrews, like practically all other peoples of the world, preferred high elevations for their worship. Many of these sites had been taken over from the Canaanites. When they could not find hills, people made artificial ones, temple mounds, pyramids, ziggurats, and structures like the heaven-storming Tower of Babel described in Genesis. In a high place, where men and women were separated from their everyday world, they seemed closer to God. This feeling is reflected in Psalm 121, "I lift up my eyes to the hills."

Saul backed away from Samuel's invitation to feast in the high place, protesting that he was unworthy of the honor. "Am I not a Benjaminite, from the least of the tribes of Israel? And is not my family the humblest of all the families of the tribe of Benjamin? Why then have you spoken to me in this way?" (I Sam. 9:21).

Though Benjamin was the smallest tribe, Saul's wealthy, land owning family was far from its humblest member. Saul, however, spoke politely in the accepted fashion of the time. His courteous words barely concealed his perplexity at his unusual reception. Why had the man of God singled out a mere stranger for such a great honor?

At the feast, Saul and his servant were given more prominent places than the thirty other guests. Saul received a special portion of the already prepared food which Samuel had told the cook to set aside. "Eat," Samuel commanded the young stranger; "because it was kept for you until the hour appointed, that you might eat with the guests" (I Sam. 9:24).

That night Saul lay down to sleep on a bed spread for him upon the roof of Samuel's house, a stranger received with mystifying honor in a city far from home.

ANOINTING OF A KING

When Saul and his servant prepared to return home, Samuel told his guest to send the servant on ahead "that I may make known to you the word of God" (I Sam. 9:27). When the two men were alone together, Samuel brought forth a special vial of holy oil. Gravely he poured it on young Saul's head and kissed him, saying, "Has not the Lord anointed you to be prince over his people Israel? And you shall reign over the people of the Lord and you will save them from the hand of their enemies round about" (I Sam. 10:1).

At last Saul knew the meaning of all the strange events that had befallen him. Three days ago he had set out from his father's house to find some lost animals. Now he stood with Israel's great prophet in the morning sun, an anointed king!

Over his head had been poured the holy oil of Israel, compounded according to a ritual formula from various ingredients: myrrh, cinnamon, aromatic cane, cassia, and olive oil. The law stated, "This shall be my holy anointing oil throughout your generations. It shall not be poured upon the bodies of ordinary men, and you shall make no other like it in composition; it is holy, and it shall be holy to you" (Exod. 30:31-32).

For the older man, the anointing action was one of high expectation only slightly shadowed by personal sadness. He had resisted Israel's plea for a king. In this solemn hour, Samuel relinquished his own office as supreme leader of Israel to a younger, very different man.

Saul had no words to say in the hour when the spirit of God was sacramentally transferred to him and "God gave him another heart" (I Sam. 10:9). Holy anointing had previously been reserved for the consecration of priests and prophets, but now kings were to be so honored. From the hour of his anointing, Saul believed himself set apart from other men as the bearer of divine inspiration.

He was told by Samuel that on his way home he would be met by "a band of prophets coming down from the high place with harp, tambourine, flute, and lyre before them, prophesying. Then the spirit of the Lord will come mightily upon you, and you shall prophesy with them and be turned into another man" (I Sam. 11:5-6). Everything happened as Samuel had said, for God's spirit came upon Saul with great power and he prophesied among the holy men.

The Greek word for this spiritual state is *enthusiasmos*, meaning "to be full of the god." Our word "enthusiastic" is derived from the Greek and conveys the idea that a person is bubbling over with excitement about something. The Hebrews, like many other ancient peoples, believed that when a man was in this state of expressive excitement called prophesying he was possessed by the divine.

There were times of enthusiasm in Saul's life when he experienced such an indwelling of God's spirit that those around him were inspired to do things that would otherwise have been impossible. It was as though a holy fire burned in him. Saul's claim to kingship was based on the objective fact of his anointing and on the subjective fact of being possessed by the spirit of God.

For a while Saul wisely said nothing to anyone about his

secret anointing. He waited for the old prophet Samuel to make the next move. Back home when Saul's uncle questioned him about his meeting with the prophet, the tall young man was noncommital, merely stating, " 'He told us plainly that the asses had been found.' But about the matter of the kingdom, of which Samuel had spoken, he did not tell him anything" (I Sam. 10:16).

ACCLAIMED KING AT MIZPAH

Not long afterward, Samuel called the tribes together in an assembly at Mizpah to determine who should be king. When lots were cast, the tribe of Benjamin was chosen, and within the tribe, the family of Matrites was singled out, and within this family, Kish's son, Saul, became the final choice.

Some scholars believe that this second story of Saul's selection as king of Israel indicates two different sources for this period of Hebrew history. This is probably true. But why did not the editor of this biblical book eliminate one of these stories? Perhaps each has its function. One story describes Samuel's personal act of prophetic election; the other, the public action of the tribes. Religion itself has these two aspects—the very private and personal, as well as the corporate, in which a man becomes part of the assembly of other believers.

At the assembly at Mizpah, Saul could not at first be found, for, as a young man, he did not take part in the solemn procedure of casting lots. He was finally found among the baggage, and when he stood up he towered above all the men of Israel.

The assembled tribes listened as Samuel introduced their new king, "Do you see him whom the Lord has chosen? There is none like him among all the people" (I Sam. 10:24). At these words a mighty shout sounded among the hills at Mizpah, "Long live the king!"

An inspired company of "men of valor whose hearts God had

touched" (I Sam. 10:26) followed their new king to his home at Gibeah. Though Saul had already won the enthusiastic loyalty of a large group, there were some Hebrews who were not present at Mizpah, and others who opposed him, doubting the validity of his claim to kingship and refusing to support him. Saul needed a dramatic victory to gain a united following.

VICTORY OVER THE AMMONITES

He soon had a chance to display his leadership. Israel's inveterate enemy, the Ammonites, raided the town of Jabesh in Gilead. There in the highlands east of the Jordan, the Ammonites made disgraceful demands on the men of Jabesh.

Messengers brought news of the insult to Saul and "the spirit of God came mightily upon Saul when he heard these words, and his anger was greatly kindled" (I Sam. 11:6). Now was the time to act so that all might know that Israel had a king capable of protecting her.

Saul sent messengers far and wide throughout the whole land of Israel, not with letters which few at that time could read, but with pieces of a yoke of oxen he had cut up. Everyone was told the meaning of these gruesome symbols. Here, said the messengers, was a sample of what would befall any man who refused to follow Saul against the Ammonites.

Thousands of Israelites answered his call. Saul divided them into three companies and led them across the Jordan to attack the Ammonite camp. So completely did the men of Israel rout the Ammonites that "those who survived were scattered, so that no two of them were left together" (I Sam. 11:11).

With this victory, Saul won acclaim from all his people. Having seen him in action, they could no longer doubt his fitness to reign. The last whispers of his opponents were drowned out by shouts of triumph.

A dream had come true. In Saul's person, the people of Israel saw a perfect union of God's sacred presence and the king's political power. With one accord the people escorted Saul to Gilgal where the monument of twelve stones from the Jordan River reminded the tribes of their basic unity. There in a solemn ceremony they renewed the kingdom and "made Saul king before the Lord in Gilgal . . . and there Saul and all the men of Israel rejoiced greatly" (I Sam. 11:15).

PHILISTINE VICTORIES

The wealthy Philistines, with their monopoly of iron-smelting, remained Israel's most dangerous threat throughout Saul's reign. Hebrew soldiers fought with stone or bronze weapons against vastly superior Philistine troops armed with iron weapons and supported by chariot corps. But Saul's brilliant leadership of the standing army he organized forged a new spirit of unity among the tribes. Israel was about to score important victories over her enemies.

The valor of Saul's son Jonathan paved the way for the first triumphs. With only his armor-bearer to support him, Jonathan attacked a Philistine outpost and succeeded in throwing their entire garrison into an uproar.

Taking advantage of the confusion, his father decided to attack the main body of Philistines. First the king sent for the priest to learn from him God's will in the matter. Before the priest could answer, however, Saul, who had been anxiously watching the enemy advance, impatiently rushed off, leading his men into battle. Joined by other Hebrews in the area, some of whom were Philistine mercenaries, Saul routed his enemy. His victory encouraged Israel, for it showed them that they no longer need bow to Philistine superiority.

into the hand of the Philistines; and tomorrow you and
shall be with me; the Lord will give the army of Israel
the hand of the Philistines" (I Sam. 28:19).

he heard the fatal message, the king was overcome and
ground in a faint. With great courage, however,
himself together, ate a meal, and strode off into the
lead his hopeless cause. Never did he seem more
majestic than in his final hours.

opes of Mount Gilboa Saul marshaled his doomed
st the Philistines. They soon attacked, killing Jona-
two brothers and pressing hard against the Israelite
his sons dead, the king fought on until wounded by
danger of capture. In the final act of his unhappy
rew his sword and fell upon it, ending his own life.
nting the deaths of mighty Saul and his valiant son
the final word about Israel's first king.

ory, O Israel, is slain upon thy high places!
are the mighty fallen! . . .

Jonathan, beloved and lovely!
and in death they were not divided;
e swifter than eagles,
ere stronger than lions.

ers of Israel, weep over Saul. . . .

he mighty fallen
weapons of war perished!

II Sam. 1:19, 23, 24, 27

STEPS TOWARD FAILURE

Saul's reign, so auspiciously begun, soon encountered trouble
of the king's own making. In his own personality and especially
in his concept of kingship lay seeds of his coming failure.

Saul and his army were stationed at Gilgal awaiting Samuel.
He was to offer a sacrifice that would prepare the Hebrews for
a coming battle. After eight days of waiting, the old prophet
still had not arrived. The troops were growing more and more
impatient, so the king decided to take matters into his own hands.
Impulsively he offered the sacrifice himself, an act only priests
were authorized to perform.

Almost immediately Samuel appeared. He refused to accept
the king's reasons for his sacrilegious act and denounced Saul for
it, saying, "You have done foolishly; you have not kept the com-
mandment of the Lord your God, which he commanded you;
for now the Lord would have established your kingdom over
Israel for ever. But now your kingdom shall not continue" (I
Sam. 13:13-14).

The point of the old prophet's denunciation was that Saul had
assumed priestly privileges not belonging to his kingly office.
Israel needed an inspired king, but not one who would make himself a priest. Furthermore, Saul had used his sacrifice as a magical
means to force God to help him in the coming battle.

Saul's failure, in this as in other cases, stemmed from grasping
too much power. With the establishment of the monarchy,
Israel's leadership was to be divided between king and priests,
reversing the old custom of entrusting all authority, both military
and spiritual, to one man. As king, Saul's duty was to lead the
tribes in worldly matters, while a priest or prophet like Samuel
would be Israel's spiritual guide. But Saul, conscious since his

anointing of being possessed by the spirit, repeatedly took upon himself priestly prerogatives.

REJECTION OF A KING

The second step in Samuel's rejection of Saul occurred after the king's victory over the Amalekites, Israel's enemy since their years in the wilderness. In the "holy" war against the Amalekites, everything Israel conquered was to be sacrificed and the enemy extinguished from the face of the earth. But Saul spared King Agag, not for humanitarian reasons, but probably to parade his conquered foe and enhance his own reputation. He also saved the best of the Amalekites' livestock.

The aging priest Samuel came into Saul's presence while he was celebrating his victory. As priest and king confronted one another, the distant bleating of the captured sheep and the lowing of the oxen could be heard. These beasts should have been sacrificed in the "holy" war, but Saul said he was keeping them for later sacrifices. Again, the king had taken sacred matters into his own hands.

The old priest, for whom obedience to God was paramount, denounced the man he had consecrated to kingship.

> Has the Lord as great delight in burnt offerings and sacrifices,
>   as in obeying the voice of the Lord?
> Behold, to obey is better than sacrifice,
>   and to hearken than the fat of rams. . . .
> Because you have rejected the word of the Lord,
>   he has also rejected you from being king.
>
> I Sam. 15:22-23

Saul bowed his head, praying for forgiveness, but Samuel would not accept his repentance and turned to leave. In desperation the king thrust forth his arm, clutching at Samuel's robe

with such force that he tore off a
his way. He would never again

When Samuel withdrew his
king a break with Hebrew r
inspiration given to Saul at h
and he began to descend into
Moods of depression, which
music of David's harp, alter
imagined were plotting agai
departed from Saul, and ar
him" (I Sam. 16:14).

The tragedy was th
Scriptural sense. He d
He was a good family
a military leader he
tribes into a cohesiv
strength.

One of the grea
breaking the Philis
Israel moved from
iron age. Withou
able to establish

On the eve
sense of forebod
long been out
the means he
he disguised h
unlawful art

This witcl
and spoke

with you
your sons
also into
When h
fell to the
he pulled
darkness t
tragically n
On the s
forces agains
than and his
army. With
archers and i
career, Saul d
David, lame
Jonathan, has

Thy gl
How

Saul and
In life
they wer
they w

Ye daugh

How are t
and the

VII

D A V I D

THE APPRENTICE KING

"ARISE, ANOINT HIM, FOR THIS IS HE"

Judged by any standards, the greatest king Israel ever had was David. As a boy watching his father's sheep on the stony Judean hills around Bethlehem, his days were spent in loneliness, far from the crowded places where men win renown. Yet news of Israel's political upheavals reached him in the remote fields where he searched for green pastures and water for his father's flocks.

One day a messenger from his father interrupted his solitary life with orders to return home. Samuel, the old priest-judge, was visiting Bethlehem in Judah and had asked to see all Jesse's sons.

At Jesse's house Samuel waited for the boy shepherd. After the Lord had rejected Saul as king over Israel, He had given Samuel the responsibility of finding and anointing a new king. This was a delicate matter to accomplish while Saul still controlled the land. But Samuel had disguised the true object of his visit to Bethlehem by offering a sacrifice with the family of Jesse. Among Jesse's sons Samuel expected to find the new leader.

One by one seven mature men came before Samuel, but the prophet knew that Israel's future king was not among them. He was careful in making his judgments, for the Lord had expressly stated, "Do not look on his appearance or on the height of his stature . . . for the Lord sees not as man sees; man looks on the outward appearance, but the Lord looks on the heart" (I Sam. 16:7). Samuel was thus forewarned not to expect to find another king as tall and handsome as Saul.

Then Samuel had asked their father, "Are all your sons here?"

Jesse replied, "There remains yet the youngest, but behold, he is keeping the sheep" (I Sam. 16:11). If his grown sons did not please the prophet, what chance had a mere shepherd lad? Still, Jesse sent for David.

When David stood before the man of God, Samuel regarded him and recognized in the ruddy youth the one for whom he searched. "And the Lord said, 'Arise, anoint him; for this is he'" (I Sam. 16:12).

With David's brothers as witnesses, Samuel poured the holy anointing oil from his horn on young David's head, consecrating him king of Israel—a fact that was to be little known as long as Saul lived. As proof of divine election, "the Spirit of the Lord came mightily upon David from that day forward" (I Sam. 16:13).

In Israel a man's right to lead was authenticated by divine inspiration. A leader did not hold his position because he came from the right family or because he received popular acclaim. Correct ritual alone could not elevate a man to the kingship. It was the Lord who made His final imprint on the man, thus setting him apart as God's deputy on earth. Israel's king was the Lord's servant.

DAVID AND GOLIATH

The encounter of David and Goliath in I Samuel 17 is the work of a master storyteller, but whether it records real history is impossible to ascertain. Though many scholars classify it as a legend or folk tale, there is a ring of truth to the whole narrative for it brings out all the unusual attributes that made David great. Symbolically then, the tale conveys the quality of David's life in a fashion that has entertained generations of listeners. From time to time the Bible uses such stories to help people understand its message.

The story of David and Goliath is a masterfully told folk tale. There is the boisterous giant who mocks the obvious fear of the Israelites. There is the freshness of David who had just left the fields of Jesse and was not burdened, as were the troops, by the weeks of frustration they had just lived through. There was David's cool handling of the slingshot, whose lethal possibilities he knew from long practice while herding.

The two armies were encamped on parallel hills, with the valley separating them. They could shout at each other, rattle their weapons, and make threats. It reminds one of the many battles described in Homeric legends or other ancient accounts. There was a lot of noise, but no action. Things turned serious when the half-grown boy without armor met the Philistine champion. "You come to me with a sword and with a spear and with a javelin; but I come to you in the name of the Lord of hosts, the God of the armies of Israel, whom you have defied. This day the Lord will deliver you into my hand . . . for the battle is the Lord's and he will give you into our hand" (I Sam. 17:45-47). And David killed Goliath.

AT SAUL'S COURT

After David's triumph, King Saul would not permit the boy to return to his father's house in Bethlehem but made him a member of the royal court. There he endeared himself to everyone, to Saul's officials and to the common people, but especially to Saul's brilliant son Jonathan. A remarkable friendship developed between the prince and young David. "The soul of Jonathan was knit to the soul of David, and Jonathan loved him as his own soul" (I Sam. 18:1). In the ancient fashion the two made a covenant, exchanging clothing and armor to seal their close bond. This friendship became vital to David's safety in the days ahead when Saul's admiration for the young hero turned to dark hatred.

David seems to have been one of those personalities about whom others cannot be neutral. He was a man people either loved deeply or genuinely hated. The Scriptures show him as he was in every aspect of life, with all his virtues and faults exposed to view. Some biblical characters appear to be black or white images with no shading, as in old woodcuts, but not David. We see him in almost true-to-life colors moving through the complexities of his day, yet always possessed of one marked ability—that of making people take a stand either for or against him and his God.

In the first flush of his incredible triumph, David rode upon a wave of popularity. When he achieved fresh victories, the women greeted him with a new popular song,

> Saul has slain his thousands,
> and David his ten thousands.
> I Sam. 18:7

This song was too much for Saul. Since his rejection by Samuel, he had lived in fear. He was no longer sure of himself and therefore no longer sure of anyone else. Jealousy caused him to both fear and hate the young man who, he believed, had stolen the love of the people, of the court, and of his son Jonathan.

In addition to his fear and anger, the Scriptures say, "When Saul saw that he had great success, he stood in awe of him" (I Sam. 18:15). Saul was aware of the connection between his own fall from grace and David's growing success. The king perhaps feared David less than he feared the hand of God.

SAUL PLOTS AGAINST DAVID

Saul had promised to give his elder daughter, Merab, as wife to the man who should overcome Goliath. When the king offered David this reward, an evil plan began to form in Saul's mind: perhaps the Philistines would make it unnecessary for him to keep his promise. "Let not my hand be upon him," schemed the king, "but let the hand of the Philistines be upon him" (I Sam. 18:17). Saul asked David to press the fight against the enemy.

While David, following royal orders, was occupied with battles, Saul gave Merab in marriage to another man.

The king's other daughter, Michal, fell in love with David. The situation offered Saul another chance to set a trap for the young warrior. David could have Michal, declared Saul, after paying a marriage price of one hundred foreskins of Philistines slain in battle, a gruesome test of valor somewhat similar to scalp hunting in American history.

To Saul's surprise, David survived his perilous mission and won the hand of Michal. But this did not end the king's hatred of David or his plots to murder him. When Jonathan learned of his father's intentions, although fully aware that David could prevent his own succession to the throne, the young prince endangered his own life to help his friend.

Michal, too, helped her husband by letting him down from a window so that he could elude the king's armed band lying in wait. Afterward she placed a dummy in David's bed to deceive Saul's officers. The dummy was an image called a *teraphim*, the same name given to the household gods Rachel stole from her father Laban. This incident doubtless reveals that idols were still revered by the Hebrews and that Israel's faith still lagged behind the requirements of the law Moses taught: "I am the Lord your God. . . . You shall have no other gods before me" (Exod. 20:2-3).

YEARS AS A FUGITIVE

No longer was it safe for David to remain at Saul's court where any moment he might be seized by the king's officers or where the royal spear could end his life. The hero became a fugitive. Soon he gathered about him a band of outlaws like himself for whom he must somehow find food.

One day David, hungry and unarmed, appeared alone at the city of Nob. He asked the priest Ahimelech for five loaves of bread for himself and his men. There was no common bread in the sanctuary, only holy bread or showbread, set out weekly in the temple. Ahimelech gave David and his followers permission to eat this sacred food on condition that they were ritually pure.

Centuries later Jesus Christ cited this incident to show that ritual laws, like the use of holy bread, are made for man, not man for the ordinances.

And he said to them, "Have you never read what David did, when he was in need and was hungry, he and those who were with him: how he entered the house of God . . . and ate the bread of the Presence, which it is not lawful for any but the priests to eat, and also gave it to those who were with him?" And he said to them, "The sabbath was made for man, not man for the sabbath." Mark 2:25-27

In the sanctuary of Nob rested a well-known trophy, Goliath's heavy iron sword wrapped in a cloth. After David had eaten and was about to leave the city, he asked for a spear or sword. Ahimelech offered the vanquished giant's great weapon, at which the young outlaw exclaimed, "There is none like that; give it to me" (I Sam. 21:9).

David fled, but the priest remained to face Saul's anger. Once more his prey had escaped him. So great was the king's wrath against Ahimelech for having helped David, that Saul ordered the priest together with his family, all the priests of the sanctuary, and the entire village of Nob massacred.

With Saul pursuing him and gaining ground, David crossed the border into Philistine territory hoping to be welcomed in Gath as an enemy of Israel's king. But the Philistines remembered the young hero's prowess all too well. Realizing his dangerous position, David pretended to be insane. Mentally ill people were not harmed because it was believed that some strange spirit worked in them. His resourcefulness enabled him to escape once again.

DAVID SPARES SAUL'S LIFE

David recruited a band of several hundred desperadoes, most of whom had good reason to live outside the law. Obviously he asked them few questions about their past misdeeds for he needed around him strong, well-armed men who would stop at nothing. He kept strict discipline among them and thus could employ men of questionable character for his purpose.

One day the outlaw band lay in the innermost recesses of the cave of Engedi, hiding from Saul who was pursuing David. The king, unaware of their presence, left his guard outside and entered the same cave. Here was the chance David's men had been waiting for. Their archenemy was easily within their grasp. But their leader kept them silent and hidden in the darkness while he stealthily approached near enough to cut off a piece of Saul's garment.

David followed Saul at a safe distance, waving his trophy and shouting,

Lo, this day your eyes have seen how the Lord gave you today into my hand in the cave; and some bade me kill you, but . . . I said, "I will not put forth my hand against my lord; for he is the Lord's

anointed." See, my father, see the skirt of your robe in my hand . . .
see that there is no wrong or treason in my hands. I have not sinned
against you, though you hunt my life to take it. . . . I Sam. 24:10-11

Saul promised to recognize David's loyalty. Afterward, however, the king's evil, suspicious mood returned, sending him out
after David again.

The king and his army encamped in the wilderness of Ziph.
Learning where Saul was, David took one companion and under
cover of darkness crept noiselessly into the camp. When they
found the king asleep with his spear planted like a standard at his
head, the companion whispered, "Let me pin him to the earth
with one stroke of the spear" (I Sam. 26:8). But David restrained
the man's arm. Instead they grabbed Saul's spear and water pitcher
and crept away from the sleeping camp.

In the morning David called across from a neighboring hill as
he lifted the royal spear, "Here is the spear, O king! . . . the
Lord gave you into my hand today, and I would not put forth
my hand against the Lord's anointed. Behold, as your life was
precious this day in my sight, so may my life be precious in the
sight of the Lord, and may he deliver me out of all tribulation"
(I Sam. 26:22-24).

Saul shouted back, "Blessed be you, my son David! You will do
many things and will succeed in them" (I Sam. 26:25). Yet this
second instance of David's loyalty did not remove Saul's enmity
against his son-in-law.

MARRIAGE TO ABIGAIL

In order to feed the band of armed men surrounding him, David
levied a toll against landholders whose flocks and herds he protected against bandits. In the highlands of southern Judea lived
Nabal whose farming and grazing lands were near Carmel. At

sheep-shearing time when David's emissaries requested food of
Nabal, citing the protection they had given his shepherds, the
landowner gave them an insolent answer. He would have no
dealings with freebooters.

"Who is David?" he asked in scorn. "Who is the son of
Jesse? . . . Shall I take my bread and my water and my meat . . .
and give it to men who come from I do not know where?"
(I Sam. 25:10-11).

Learning of Nabal's reply, David gave the signal to his band,
"Every man gird on his sword!"

One of Nabal's men reported the matter to his wife Abigail,
a beautiful woman of rare spirit and wisdom. She quickly and
efficiently took matters into her own hands, realizing that the
outlaw leader might indeed bring evil against her husband and
all his house and that Nabal was too stubborn and ill-natured
to be reasoned with. She knew that someone like David might
one day be victorious.

She packed bountiful gifts on the backs of asses: "two hundred
loaves, and two skins of wine, and five sheep ready dressed, and
five measures of parched grain, and a hundred clusters of raisins,
and two hundred cakes of figs" (I Sam. 25:18). Then she set out
in haste to intercept David and his men.

As soon as she met David, she alighted from her mount and
fell at his feet, pleading forgiveness for her husband's rudeness
and begging the young outlaw to spare her home.

The outlaw chief accepted her gifts. "Go up in peace to your
house," he gently told her; "see, I have hearkened to your voice,
and I have granted your petition" (I Sam. 25:35).

Abigail's story does not end here, for after the sudden death
of her husband, David courted her. Within a short time the two
were man and wife. Despite harrowing moments in his outlaw
years, David's early life contained its share of romance.

The Scriptures report almost casually that he soon took another wife, Ahinoam of Jezreel in the north. Abigail was from the south and Saul's daughter, Michal, David's first wife, was from the center of Israel. His marriages appear to have been a pleasant mixture of politics and love.

TRAINING AS A POLITICIAN

David showed signs from the beginning of becoming a great politician. He was shrewd, knowing when to wait and when to act quickly. He was able to subordinate practically everything to his ambition. Even his family, his wives and friends—and honesty itself—he was willing at times to place below his prime objective. Like every real politician, he lived under an obsession, partly a drive to self-fulfillment, partly an honest desire to serve his people.

The stories of David show his ability to adjust to any situation, turning it to his own advantage. Without losing sight of his goal he was all things to all people. He feigned madness, when it was necessary; he was loyal, when it was necessary; he wooed the enemy, when it was necessary. He knew he was anointed to be king and he meant to be king.

Toward the end of his long and difficult apprenticeship, when he was still at an impasse with Saul, David again offered his services as a mercenary to the Philistines. This time they accepted him. He and his men were established in the remote Philistine village of Ziklag on the southern border of Judah. From here the Philistines thought he was earning the undying hatred of Israel by raiding their towns. Actually he and his men were raiding such inveterate enemies of Israel as the Amalekites and, unknown to the Philistines, making gifts of the spoils of war to the elders of Israel. This campaign David cleverly used to influence those who might one day support him as king.

David was far away at Ziklag when Israel's tall king fought and fell at Mount Gilboa. The Philistines still did not trust the young outlaw sufficiently to use him in battle against his own people, so he was spared the awful decision to draw his sword as a Philistine mercenary against Israel in Saul's last battle.

ON THE EVE OF KINGSHIP

David did not take over a strong kingdom. Saul had been successful in establishing an army able to oppose the Philistines, but many of his men fell in his disastrous last battle. Saul welded the tribes into a nation, yet Israel lacked central taxation and a national policy. Though their first king forged the Hebrews into an effective working unit, it remained for the second to make the kingdom secure.

David was no longer an innocent country boy as on the day of his anointing. His years under Saul, in good times and in bad, had trained him for power. He was not simply thrust unprepared upon the throne, as Saul had been. Nothing but his initial anointing was handed to him. He had to fight for every step in his growth. That was why his people loved him. They could see that he was indeed one of them while at the same time he was above them in gifts and destiny.

IX

DAVID

ISRAEL'S GREATEST KING

"Where do you come from?" David asked the weary runner.

"I have escaped from the camp of Israel," replied the Amalekite messenger, a mercenary from Saul's army.

"How did the battle go at Mount Gilboa?" demanded David, who had waited three days at Ziklag for news from the north.

The Amalekite gave his report. "The people have fled from the battle, and many of the people also have fallen and are dead; and Saul also and his son Jonathan are also dead" (II Sam. 1:4).

David pressed the soldier for details of the disaster. "How did it happen? How do you know?"

The messenger told his story.

By chance I happened to be on Mount Gilboa; and there was Saul leaning upon his spear; and lo, the chariots and the horsemen were close upon him. And when he looked behind him, he saw me, and called to me. And I answered, "Here I am." . . . And he said to me, "Stand beside me and slay me; for anguish has seized me, and yet my life still lingers." So I stood beside him, and slew him, because I was sure that he could not live after he had fallen; and I took the crown which was on his head and the armlet which was on his arm, and I have brought them here to my lord.   II Sam. 1:6-10

one empire. The fatal split between north and south opened once more in the reign of Solomon's unwise and haughty son Rehoboam.

After Saul's death his surviving son Ishbosheth was declared king of "Israel," meaning the territory of the ten northern tribes. Saul's capable general, Abner, supported Ishbosheth. This military man, planning to control the northern tribes, took one of Saul's concubines. This action made Abner powerful in Hebrew eyes because it meant he now occupied the king's bed. David acted in a similar manner. His price for peace with the north was the return of his former wife Michal, Saul's daughter, who had been given to someone else when he became an outlaw.

Despite the relatively low social standing of women in Hebrew society, their relationship to a king often helped to determine the status of their husbands.

CONFLICT BETWEEN TWO GENERALS

David chose an able general named Joab to oppose Abner. The king certainly made use of Joab's capabilities, but he obviously came to dislike his "chief of staff," cursing him and expressing his dislike on many occasions.

Joab seems to have been a man of violent temper. When his brother was killed in the ugly struggle between north and south, he determined to avenge the death.

At this time David received Abner at Hebron, hoping to end the senseless killings. The northern general had fallen out with Ishbosheth and decided to transfer the allegiance of the ten northern tribes to David. He promised the king, "I will . . . gather all Israel to my lord the king, that they may make a covenant with you, and that you may reign over all that your heart desires" (II Sam. 3:21).

David welcomed this offer and sent Abner away in peace. Trusting in the king's word, Abner was perhaps less careful than usual and saw nothing suspicious in Joab's request to speak with him. Suddenly, to avenge his brother, Joab turned on Abner and treacherously killed him. The general's death actually hastened peace between the warring northern and southern tribes, but David felt uneasy about the outrage and did not want Joab too near him; God's curse for a broken oath might fall on him.

With or without David's consent, the weeding out by murder continued. The king acted in the accepted fashion of the time to achieve his goal of the unification of the Hebrews. Finally all the tribes gathered at Hebron and declared, "Behold we are your bone and flesh . . . and the Lord said to you, 'You shall be shepherd of my people Israel, and you shall be prince over Israel' " (II Sam. 5:1-2).

After a seven-year reign over Judah and Benjamin from his capital of Hebron, David at the age of thirty was anointed by the elders of Israel to reign over all the tribes. His entire reign would last forty years.

JERUSALEM HIS CAPITAL

David needed a neutral capital for the united tribes and one more central than the southern city of Hebron. The Jebusites had occupied Jerusalem up to this time, resisting all Hebrew attempts to take the coveted city. But David finally succeeded in capturing the fortress there, the Mount of Zion. He rebuilt it, strengthened its fortifications, and moved his court and elite guard to Jerusalem.

The name of Hiram, King of Tyre is mentioned for the first time in connection with David's building operations. "And Hiram king of Tyre sent messengers to David, and cedar trees, also carpenters and masons who built David a house" (II Sam. 5:11). The record indicates international recognition for David's reign, for Phoenician rulers like Hiram did not engage in political and economic relationships unless they were sure of the power and the credit of the other party.

BRINGING THE ARK TO JERUSALEM

To ensure that everyone acknowledged Mount Zion as the true capital of Israel, David proposed to install the Ark of the Covenant there, thus making Jerusalem the dwelling-place of God. The sacred symbol had remained under shelter at Kiriath-jearim in the house of Abinadab since the disastrous battles of Samuel's time. With a large company of chosen men, David "carried the ark of God upon a new cart, and brought it out of the house of Abinadab which was on the hill. . . . And David and all the house of Israel were making merry before the Lord with all their might, with songs and lyres, and harps and tambourines and castanets and cymbals" (II Sam. 6:3-5).

The transport of this religious object was a difficult task, for the Hebrews had forgotten how to handle it. When the Ark was finally brought in great pomp up the mountain road to Jerusalem the people shouted and blew trumpets. In an ecstasy of religious fervor, "David danced before the Lord with all his might; and David was girded with a linen ephod" (II Sam. 6:14).

David's wife Michal did share her husband's joy over the restoration of the Ark to Israel, but she did not approve of his dancing. She told him he was no better than a common rake shamelessly exposing himself as he performed his ecstatic dance clad only in the linen ephod. But David brushed aside her scolding, knowing that the common people would understand his exuberance as genuine love of the Lord. "I will be abased in your eyes;" he said, "but by the maids of whom you have spoken, by them I shall be held in honor" (II Sam. 6:22).

Here is an instance of the mixture of politics and religion

so characteristic of David. His joy before the Lord was real, but it was also a good "show" for the common people who wanted their king to display the sign of the spirit.

CONSOLIDATING HIS KINGDOM

The chief military and political achievements of David are summarized in II Samuel 8, though some later important conquests are not included. Israel's old enemy, the Philistines, were driven back to a small coastal strip from which they were not able to mount a major attack against David's army. The four nations of Ammon, Moab, Edom, and Amalek were either annexed to David's empire by treaty, held as vassal states, or administered by military governors. The area of Zobah north of Damascus with its Aramaean, or as we would say, Syrian population, was brought under David's rule, establishing Israel's contact with the Phoenicians on the northern coast. Both the king and his son Solomon maintained friendly relations with this powerful maritime nation.

David knew, as have many other strong leaders in history, that it is wise for a king to keep himself somewhat apart from the people by a wall of hired men sworn to no other allegiance. The men of David's bodyguard are called Cherethites and Pelethites in the English Bible, names that are variations for "Cretans" and "Philistines."

The king was now secure on Israel's throne. There still remained one survivor of Saul's family, Jonathan's crippled son, Mephibosheth. Dropped in childhood by his nurse as they fled after the disaster at Mount Gilboa, Mephibosheth was lame in both feet. This pathetic descendant of royalty posed no threat to his dynastic ambitions, so David decided to gain additional popular support by inviting Mephibosheth to his court in Jerusalem.

"Do not fear," said David to Jonathan's son, "for I will show

you kindness for the sake of your father Jonathan, and I will restore to you all the land of Saul your father; and you shall eat at
my table always" (II Sam. 9:7).

It was a gesture calculated to show the people of Israel that
David's reign followed Saul's smoothly and without reprisal.

For the moment everything was going well for David. All his
major enemies had been overcome and none of the great world
powers of the future had yet arisen. David's word was law
throughout a wide empire inhabited by many subject peoples.
Yet at the very heart of his success lurked a danger. Could
he wield his great power without being corrupted by it? Would
success go to his head, convincing him that he could have anything he wanted?

BATHSHEBA AND DAVID

It was spring, "the time when kings go forth to battle" (II Sam.
11:1). David had sent his general Joab to besiege the Ammonite
town of Rabbah while he remained in the new palace he had built
in Jerusalem. It was also the time when romance is in the air.

It happened, late one afternoon, when David . . . was walking upon
the roof of the king's house, that he saw from the roof a woman bathing; and the woman was very beautiful. And David sent and inquired
about the woman. And one said, "Is not this Bathsheba . . . the wife of
Uriah the Hittite?" So David sent messengers, and took her. . . . And
the woman conceived; and she sent and told David, "I am with child."

II Sam. 11:2-5

To cover up the scandal, the king sent for Uriah, who was
one of his army commanders serving under Joab. David hoped
to make it seem that Uriah was the father of Bathsheba's unborn
child. But the plan did not succeed. Uriah refused to break the
strict rules of a consecrated soldier in holy warfare and would

not visit his wife. The loyal warrior believed that by such be-
havior he would betray his hard-pressed comrades-in-arms as they
laid siege to Rabbah.

When Uriah insisted on returning to the battlefield, David put
into the man's hands his own death warrant. It was a letter to
Joab in which the king instructed his general, "Set Uriah in the
forefront of the hardest fighting, and then draw back from him,
that he may be struck down and die" (II Sam. 11:15).

The Ammonites made a savage attack and Uriah fell. The
message the king sent Joab after Uriah's death had a hollow
sound, "Do not let this matter trouble you, for the sword devours
now one and now another" (II Sam. 11:25).

After Bathsheba had dutifully gone through mourning ceremonies for her slain husband, David brought her to his house. She
became his wife and bore him a son. Would no one dare raise
his voice in protest against the king for taking Uriah's wife and
plotting his death?

"YOU ARE THE MAN"

Then something surprising happened, an event that would not
have taken place in any other oriental nation, of that time or later.
With matchless courage Nathan the prophet confronted King
David.

Nathan told a story about two men, supposedly because he
wanted the king's legal advice in the matter. One of the men
was rich in flocks and herds, but the other was poor, owning just
one ewe lamb that grew up as a household pet with the man's
children. She ate his food, drank from his cup, and nestled in his
arms. The poor man loved her as a daughter. Yet one day the
rich man, wishing to honor a visitor with a banquet, decided not
to take one of his own animals, but to slaughter the poor man's
ewe lamb instead.

David's response to this tale was what Nathan hoped. He announced his royal opinion angrily, "As the Lord lives, the man who has done this deserves to die; and he shall restore the lamb fourfold, because he did this thing, and because he had no pity" (II Sam. 12:5-6).

The prophet advanced, pointed to David, and said, "You are the man" (II Sam. 12:7).

Thus says the Lord, the God of Israel. . . . "Why have you despised the word of the Lord to do what is evil in his sight? You have smitten Uriah the Hittite with the sword, and have taken his wife to be your wife. . . . Now therefore the sword shall never depart from your house. . . . Behold, I will raise up evil against you out of your own house."   II Sam. 12:7-11

In words that reveal a deep sense of guilt and penitence he said to Nathan, "I have sinned against the Lord" (II Sam. 12:13).

Nathan uttered the Lord's forgiveness, but declared that punishment would fall on David, for the son born to him and Bathsheba would die.

DEATH OF A YOUNG PRINCE

When Bathsheba's young son became fatally ill, David fasted and prayed. But after the child died, David, a realist even in the intimate affairs of his private life, anointed himself, changed his clothes, and broke his fast. His servants were surprised, for they thought the father should be grieving for his dead son. But David said,

While the child was still alive, I fasted and wept; for I said, "Who knows whether the Lord will be gracious to me, that the child may live?" But now he is dead; why should I fast? Can I bring him back again? I shall go to him, but he will not return to me.

II Sam. 12:22-23

Before long Bathsheba was comforted by the birth of another child, Solomon. This was the son destined to be David's successor —a distinction indeed, in view of the king's numerous wives and concubines and the many children claiming David as their father.

ABSALOM'S TREACHERY

The latter years of the king's life were disturbed by family troubles, as Nathan had predicted. There was discontent among his sons. From the standpoint of his impatient heirs, David's reign lasted far too long.

The son most hostile to David was Absalom, a young man with a magnetism that attracted a devoted following. Apparently he was the king's favorite, for David recognized in his brilliance something of his own political skill and his ability to lead. Even after Absalom ordered his older brother Amnon killed, he managed to work his way back into David's court. Soon he stirred up a rebellion against the old king. So cleverly was it planned and so perfect were the preparations that when the revolt erupted, David was forced to flee from Jerusalem. He left the city with his head covered, dodging stones hurled by his enemies.

As the king fled in disgrace, Shimei, of the tribe of Benjamin and a relative of Saul's, cursed David. But the king would not let his tormentor be harmed, saying, "Behold my own son seeks my life; how much more now may this Benjaminite! Let him alone, and let him curse; for the Lord has bidden him" (II Sam. 16:11).

Thus David let go all false pride, all pretenses. In his heart he knew how much of this calamity he deserved. This kind of humility reveals David's tremendous inner strength.

Ten women of David's harem, his wives and concubines who remained in Jerusalem, Absalom planned to make his own in order to show the people that he was really David's successor. He had popular support; he controlled Jerusalem; he had some of the king's women. Was he not already the king?

In the forest of Ephraim a battle was fought between David's loyal men and Absalom's rebels. Riding through the forest on his mule, Absalom was caught by his long hair in the branches of a great oak tree. He was left helplessly hanging when his mule ran off from under him. David's commander Joab found him thus and slew the young traitor, knowing that an enemy of the state and of the king had to die.

Once again David watched for a messenger bringing news of battle. Soon came one named Ahimaaz, son of a priest, announcing "All is well." The rebellion had failed and all the rebels had been captured. But David did not rejoice. Anxiously he asked Ahimaaz, "Is it well with the young man Absalom?" (II Sam. 18:29).

Learning of his rebellious son's death, the desolate king could not be comforted with the thought that he had regained his kingdom. All he could cry in his heartbroken anguish was, "O my son Absalom, my son, my son Absalom! Would I had died instead of you, O Absalom, my son, my son!" (II Sam. 18:33).

THE ROYAL SUCCESSION

Uprisings and discontent made it necessary to guard the old king carefully in his last years.

Even Bathsheba, no longer young and beautiful, now had to knock at his door and humbly ask for an interview. The old man was ministered to by a beautiful young nurse, Abishag the Shunammite. Finally Nathan the prophet arranged by clever intrigue for the king to transfer his royal power to Bathsheba's son Solomon. David commissioned Nathan:

Take with you the servants of your lord, and cause Solomon my son to ride on my own mule, and bring him down to Gihon; and let Zadok the priest and Nathan the prophet there anoint him king over

Israel; then blow the trumpet, and say, "Long live King Solomon!" You shall then come up after him, and he shall come and sit upon my throne; for he shall be king in my stead.   I Kings 1:33-35

Before he died, David addressed Solomon in a moving farewell. "I am about to go the way of all the earth. Be strong, and show yourself a man, and keep the charge of the Lord your God, walking in his ways . . ." (I Kings 2:2-3). It was typical of him that the honor of his throne, the preservation of the dynasty, and his own reputation as a king were uppermost in his mind. At the last, he showed little love or forgiveness for he warned Solomon of old grudges and potential enemies and advised him to cut them down.

When David died, they buried him in Jerusalem where his son was already reigning. The forty-year rule of this clever politician and powerful king included many sinful acts. Nowhere in the Scriptures is there any better example than the life of Israel's greatest king that God works through sinners to accomplish His purposes.

X

SOLOMON
THE BUILDER

GAINING A KINGDOM

In the valley below Jerusalem there is a spring called Gihon which in ancient times supplied water to the city. At this place Solomon was anointed king to the sound of great rejoicing.

There Zadok the priest took the horn of oil from the tent, and anointed Solomon. Then they blew the trumpet; and all the people said, "Long live King Solomon!" And all the people went up after him, playing on pipes, and rejoicing with great joy, so that the earth was split with their noise.   I Kings 1:39-40

Not far away, Solomon's older brother, Adonijah, was feasting with his friends and supporters when he heard the noise. Up to this time Adonijah had been sure that, because he was David's oldest surviving son, he would surely inherit his father's throne. Such a succession would be according to dynastic rules. Moreover, he enjoyed the support not only of many of the people, but of such well-known court figures as David's general, Joab, and the priest, Abiathar.

Unknown to Adonijah his claims to kingship were being undermined by a small but influential court group that was maneuvering to place Solomon on the throne. Foremost among the plotters were Solomon's mother Bathsheba, Nathan the prophet, and Benaiah, who commanded David's bodyguard of Cherethites and Pelethites. As we have already noted in the last chapter, Bathsheba's wishes carried great weight with the aged David. The king also heeded Nathan, for it was believed that the Lord spoke through him to Israel, a nation still faithful to the spiritual element in her kingship.

Adonijah's alert supporter Joab heard the sound of people rejoicing at Gihon and asked, "What does this uproar in the city mean?" (I Kings 1:41).

When a messenger rushed in to the feast, Adonijah welcomed him hopefully: "You bring us good news!"

"No," replied the young man, "for our lord King David has made Solomon king . . . the city is in an uproar. This is the noise that you have heard. Solomon sits upon the royal throne" (I Kings 1:43, 45-46).

Such an event often brought bloodshed, even as it does today in some parts of the world. So Adonijah, fearing for his life, fled to the sanctuary where he clung to the horns of the altar. According to the rights of refuge, he was safe from pursuers there.

Learning of his older brother's fear of him, Solomon magnanimously declared that if Adonijah proved loyal to him not a hair of his head would be harmed. The new king wanted to begin his reign by conciliating as many of his rivals and enemies as possible.

Adonijah, however, was unable to accept his younger brother's sovereignty. He attempted a counter-move. After his father's death, he asked Bathsheba to intercede for him to obtain Abishag, David's former Shunammite nurse, as his wife. Probably Adonijah was attempting to gain power by establishing himself in the royal bed, as on other occasions Abner and Absalom had tried to do.

Quick to sense a bid for power in his older brother's request,

Solomon sent for his military commander, Benaiah, and, despite previous assurances to Adonijah, ordered his brother put to death.

ESTABLISHING HIS KINGDOM

Who else threatened Solomon's sway? Both Abiathar the priest and Joab the general had supported the murdered Adonijah. Swiftly Solomon moved to quell any attempt on their part to rebel. Solomon could be reasonably sure that, with the prince Adonijah dead, the priest would cause no trouble. But to be safe, Solomon exiled him to his home in Anathoth. The king then appointed one of his own followers as chief priest in Jerusalem— Zadok, who had anointed him at Gihon.

In pronouncing his sentence of banishment, Solomon said to Abiathar,

Go to Anathoth, to your estate; for you deserve death. But I will not at this time put you to death, because you bore the ark of the Lord God before David my father, and because you shared in all the affliction of my father.   I Kings 2:26

With Joab, Adonijah's other supporter, Solomon was not as merciful. The king knew of the difficulties his father had had with the fiery, headstrong general who had taken the murder of Abner into his own hands. Realizing that his loyalty could never be depended on, Solomon decided to kill him. Though Joab fled to the sanctuary and caught hold of the horns of the altar, Benaiah pursued him and struck him down, as he had Adonijah. This time the traditional right of sanctuary was not honored.

Benaiah was rewarded for these two executions by being made commander-in-chief of Israel's army in Joab's place.

Before Solomon could feel secure on this throne, he had to deal with a man of the family of Saul, Shimei, who had cursed David.

The king put Shimei under house arrest in Jerusalem, but when he broke this to go on a highly suspicious journey to Gath, Solomon ordered Benaiah to kill him.

CHARACTER OF SOLOMON'S REIGN

Toward the end of David's life, the court at Jerusalem developed along oriental lines. In this we see fulfilled the people's desire to pattern themselves after their neighbors. The Hebrews, in losing their "separateness," had gained in culture and civilization, but their political structure remained still closely tied to their religious faith.

Solomon was a different sort of man from his father. David had come up through the ranks. He had made his own way, living by his wits as an exile, forging an empire out of the opportunities presented to him. His trials molded his strong personality, giving him a deeply religious bent.

Much of this struggle and testing was denied Solomon, who was born, as it were, with a silver spoon in his mouth. He expected to be served. He had never had to work for what he had. Even the kingdom was virtually presented to him by his mother and by Nathan, Zadok, and Benaiah.

From the accounts of his reign, Solomon's chief concern seems to have been the power of his luxurious court. We are told that he had seven hundred wives and three hundred concubines. These astonishing numbers indicate Solomon's shrewd political expediency more than anything else, for the women of his harem were more hostages than wives, and the weddings, political acts to assure peace. As David had done in the previous reign, and as European royal houses did into modern times, Solomon ratified treaties of alliance by marrying the daughters of foreign rulers.

Thus, "Solomon made a marriage alliance with Pharaoh king

of Egypt; he took Pharaoh's daughter, and brought her into the city of David" (I Kings 3:1). Later he built a costly palace for this foreign princess who, among all his wives, seems to have been accorded the highest honors, as befitted one whose father ruled the kingdom on the Nile.

But many royal ladies vied for position at Solomon's court. There were highborn women from other nations, "Moabite, Ammonite, Edomite, Sidonian, and Hittite women, from the nations concerning which the Lord had said to the people of Israel, 'You shall not enter into marriage with them . . . for surely they will turn away your heart after their gods'; Solomon clung to these in love" (I Kings 11:1-2).

Solomon's court thus included his numerous wives and their attendants, as well as courtiers and officials. All ate at the royal table. When the Queen of Sheba visited him in Jerusalem and saw "the house that he had built, the food of his table, the seating of his officials, and the attendance of his servants, their clothing, his cupbearers . . . there was no more spirit in her" (I Kings 10:4-5). Yet she was a ruler accustomed to no little luxury herself. A record of food provided for Solomon's court includes, as a daily allowance, "thirty cors of fine flour, and sixty cors of meal, ten fat oxen, and twenty pasture-fed cattle, a hundred sheep, besides harts, gazelles, roebucks, and fatted fowl" (I Kings 4:22-23).

ADMINISTRATION OF HIS KINGDOM

To maintain the splendor of his court and the might of his standing army, Solomon imposed heavy taxation and exacted forced labor. For taxation purposes he subdivided his empire into twelve districts, only five of which showed any resemblance to the old tribal areas. The king apparently designed the new districts to break down former tribal loyalties and integrate all separate forces into one nation under central authority.

In the beginning of the reign, before taxation or the labor levies had become burdensome, "Judah and Israel were as many as the sand by the sea; they ate and drank and were happy" (I Kings 4:20). But this idyllic situation did not long continue.

It is true that Solomon's was an empire of peace. He was able to build on the military successes of his father and to extend his influence over a wide territory, ruling "over all the kingdoms from the Euphrates to the land of the Philistines and to the border of Egypt" (I Kings 4:21). Solomon engaged in few wars with major powers, for Egypt had made peace with Israel and the Assyrian empire in the north was still in process of formation. Thus the king was able to concentrate his attention and most of his energy on the internal affairs of his kingdom.

Many impressive remains of Solomon's empire have been unearthed by archaeologists. They have discovered some of the numerous garrisons he established from which his greatly enlarged standing army, with its improved equipment, was able to impose the king's will on all parts of the empire.

His excavated stables at Megiddo testify to the great numbers of horses and chariots ready to carry out Solomon's orders. In Megiddo alone, which was only one city in the king's chain of defenses, no less than five hundred horses could be stabled at a time. Solomon's policy was one of preparedness. He relied on powerful mobile forces that could be quickly deployed against an enemy, or used as a police force within Israel. He left nothing to chance.

BUILDING OPERATIONS

The greatest achievement of Solomon's reign was the building up of Jerusalem and the erection of a temple within its walls. The latter project had been close to David's heart, but he had had to leave it to his son. At the outset Solomon faced three needs for his ambitious projects: craftsmen, materials, and labor.

Israel had been a seminomadic people up to the time of Samuel, with little opportunity to develop an artistic style or a distinctive architecture of her own. In the three reigns of Saul, David, and Solomon, the Hebrew people had passed rapidly from the stone age to the iron age. To any man who had managed to reach the age of seventy-five in Solomon's time, the world of his boyhood had been transformed almost beyond belief.

In the arts, Israel was backward. This was owing in part to the rapidity of her development and to her policy of exterminating the Canaanites with their more advanced civilization, their high level of artistic achievement, and their superior craftsmen.

When Solomon began to build Jerusalem's temple many of the remaining Canaanites were concentrated in the northern area called Phoenicia. Consequently the king of Israel had to apply to the ruler of Phoenicia for craftsmen able to erect elaborate buildings. Thus Solomon's temple was constructed according to Phoenician plans adapted to the needs of Israel's religion. This meant that Canaanite architectural ideas and decorative symbols were used in the new buildings.

Phoenicia also supplied timber for rebuilding Jerusalem. On the slopes of Mount Lebanon, the hundred-mile long mountain range of Phoenicia's hinterland, grew dense forests of magnificent cedar trees. Remnants of these ancient forests with their fragrant, long-lived trees still survive in the modern Republic of Lebanon. Phoenician foresters, working with gangs of Solomon's laborers, cut the cedar and also the firs of Lebanon. From the mountain sides the logs were taken down to the seacoast, lashed together into rafts and floated south to the port of Joppa. From there they were laboriously hauled overland to Jerusalem. Solomon paid King Hiram of Tyre for this timber with foodstuffs grown in Israel.

At first Solomon drew his laborers from weaker neighboring nations or foreigners living in Israel. But the requirements of his vast projects became too great, and soon he drew upon his own people. Each month thousands of Hebrews were forced to work in the forests of Lebanon. The laborers were then permitted two months at home, after which they returned to the forests for another month's service. In this way one fourth of each year was spent in forced labor for the king—a very heavy burden on the people.

It is not certain what kind of stone was used for the temple. Today the so-called "stone of the kings" is being cut by modern masons from quarries close to Jerusalem. This stone of marble-like composition is very resistant to weathering and turns into a golden yellow of impressive beauty. It is possible that Solomon's laborers worked these same quarries.

THE TEMPLE

Like Canaanite temples, the sanctuary Solomon erected in Jerusalem consisted of three parts: vestibule, nave, and Holy of Holies. The whole stone structure, only about one hundred feet long and thirty feet wide, was surrounded by a great open court in which stood the bronze altar of sacrifice and a huge bronze basin capable of holding more than ten thousand gallons of water.

The metal basin, called "the molten sea" (I Kings 7:23), was supported on the backs of twelve bronze bulls. Their presence, as well as the ornamental work mentioned in I Kings 6, shows that a significant change was emerging in Israel's faith. In the Ten Commandments Moses had forbidden "a graven image, or any likeness of anything that is in heaven above, or that is in the earth beneath, or that is in the water under the earth" (Exod. 20:4).

The bronze bulls and ornamentation indicate the acceptance of religious imagery rejected by Israel long before at Mount Sinai when Moses destroyed the golden calf.

The description of the temple proves that foreign religious ideas and symbolism had invaded Israel's faith. The comparative simplicity of the old-time worship of Yahweh seemed to have disappeared. Was the exclusive God of Israel to be placed in the company of the hierarchy of gods worshiped throughout the Fertile Crescent?

FAITH IN YAHWEH PREVAILS

When the Ark of the Covenant was brought into the temple, the old faith in Yahweh triumphed. The Ark was carried on two poles across the open court. It passed between the two bronze pillars called Jachin and Boaz which guarded the entrance to the vestibule and advanced through the long incense-filled nave. This was a room sixty feet long, wainscoted and floored with cedar. Finally, the Ark was reverently placed in the small, inmost room of the sanctuary, the completely dark, windowless Holy of Holies. Two golden cherubim covered the Ark with their wings. Inside the sacred chest was nothing "except the two tables of stone which Moses put there at Horeb, where the Lord made a covenant with the people of Israel, when they came out of the land of Egypt" (I Kings 8:9).

Empty of everything but the Ark, the austere Holy of Holies clearly proved that Israel had not wholly abandoned her ancient faith. None of the idols of neighboring peoples were set up in Israel's most holy place. In spite of the encroachment of alien religions, Solomon still maintained the basic convictions of the Hebrews.

When the Ark was brought into the most holy place, the glory and majesty of God seemed to be resting on it. Though Solomon later clarified his idea, his opening words at the dedication seem to reflect the belief that God actually dwelt in the building he had erected. The king said,

> The Lord has set the sun in the heavens,
>   but has said that he would dwell in thick darkness.
> I have built thee an exalted house,
>   a place for thee to dwell in for ever.
>   I Kings 8:12-13

Solomon's prayer at the dedication of the temple (I Kings 8:22-53) began with an overwhelming preoccupation with himself and his dynasty. He reminded the God of Israel that all this splendor of cut stone, carved wood, and cast bronze was erected to the glory of His name only because He had made such generous promises to David.

But the king moved on to express the authentic religious insight of the classical Hebrew faith. In spite of the magnificence of the building before him, the king knew that God did not dwell there, for He is too great to be held by any man-made thing.

"But will God indeed dwell on earth?" asked Solomon. "Behold, heaven and the highest heaven cannot contain thee; how much less this house which I have built! Yet have regard to the prayer of thy servant . . . yea, hear thou in heaven thy dwelling place . . ." (I Kings 8:27-28, 30).

The prayer concluded with his recognition of Israel's special place in history. "For thou didst separate them from among all the peoples of the earth, to be thy heritage . . . when thou didst bring our fathers out of Egypt, O Lord God" (I Kings 8:53). From then on Israel would have to live with this ever-present tension—to be separate and yet at the same time to be like all the nations.

DECLINE

From this high moment, Solomon's reign headed toward decline. There were many contributing factors. One was the forced labor and heavy taxation required for his extensive projects. We note that the king spent seven years building the temple with its elaborate furnishings and thirteen years building his palace and the structures needed for his harem. This meant that the people of Israel were subjected to at least twenty years of economic drain and compulsory labor. Israel paid a steep price for the glory of Solomon's empire.

Another factor was the introduction of foreign religions. When Solomon's wives and concubines burned incense and sacrificed to other gods, the king could not object, for these women represented important foreign powers. As their presence in Jerusalem guaranteed his alliances and treaties with neighboring peoples, Solomon had to mollify his wives by building sanctuaries to their gods. Though Yahweh's temple stood on Jerusalem's highest hill, buildings dedicated to his wives' gods were erected on lesser hills. Nor was this all. Solomon carried his appeasement one step too far by himself worshiping with his wives at their various shrines. Thus he set aside Yahweh's exclusiveness, earning the estimate of him recorded in the Scriptures, "For when Solomon was old his wives turned away his heart after other gods; and his heart was not wholly true to the Lord his God, as was the heart of David his father" (I Kings 11:4).

Trouble on Israel's southern and northern borders caused concern in Jerusalem. Hadad the Edomite, with the help of the Egyptians, harried the southern part of Solomon's kingdom, while the rebellious Rezon in the north endangered the king's rule over Syria. The most serious trouble, however, developed internally.

Jeroboam, an able, industrious young man, became a favorite of the king, who put him in charge of a section of the labor force. But the prophet Ahijah, realizing the growing weakness of Solomon's kingdom and the unusual promise and popularity of Jeroboam, saw greater possibilities for the young man than his present position of overseer of forced labor.

One day, in typical prophetic fashion, Ahijah performed a symbolic act. The prophet found Jeroboam on the road and when the two men were alone, Ahijah took his new robe and dramatically tore it into twelve pieces. It was intended to show that Yahweh would tear Solomon's kingdom apart. Then he said to the young man, "Take for yourself ten pieces; for thus says the Lord, the God of Israel, 'Behold, I am about to tear the kingdom from the hand of Solomon, and will give you ten tribes . . . because he has forsaken me . . .'" (I Kings 11:31, 33).

The prophet's announcement came true, for when Solomon's son Rehoboam succeeded to his father's throne, a revolution split his kingdom in two. The ten northern tribes formed a separate nation of their own under Jeroboam's leadership, while only Judah and Benjamin remained loyal to the house of David.

HIS WISDOM

Though his domestic policies weakened Israel and laid the groundwork for a divided empire, Solomon is credited with great wisdom. Any oriental potentate of the period wanted to be the most learned and wisest man in the world, as well as the mightiest and the richest, and to possess the most magnificent palace and the largest harem. In his desires, Solomon resembled other rulers, just as he emulated them in many of the goals he pursued to "put Israel on the map."

But there is some evidence for the soundness of his judgment. One of his good policies was to close the many small sanctuaries exposed to pagan influences throughout the land. He concentrated all worship of Yahweh in the new temple in Jerusalem. This meant that scholars and writers flocked to the capital city where the nation's archives were stored. The elaborate ritual of the temple required a skilled and numerous priesthood, trained, no doubt, in a central school. Here, too, the many officials needed for Solomon's far-flung enterprises must have been trained. Centralization of worship and government were wise moves on Solomon's part.

His trade policies were also very clever. At Ezion-geber, the so-called "Pittsburgh of Israel" on the Gulf of Aqaba, a northern arm of the Red Sea, Solomon built, in a joint venture with Hiram of Tyre, a fleet of ships manned by Phoenician seamen. These sturdy, flat-bottomed vessels, equipped with oars and sails, won for Solomon a profitable share of the eastern maritime trade. They carried iron and copper mined from rich deposits in the Negev and the Arabah and refined in the large smelting plant he built at Ezion-geber. On their homeward voyage the vessels brought exotic cargoes: "gold, silver, ivory, apes, and peacocks" (I Kings 10:22).

Situated on the caravan routes between Egypt and Asia Minor, Solomon's kingdom profited from trade in horses and chariots. The highly-developed chariot industry of Egypt sold its products to Solomon's merchants as did the men of Kue (Cilicia) who bred pedigreed war horses. "A chariot could be imported from Egypt for six hundred shekels of silver, and a horse for a hundred and fifty; and so through the king's traders they were exported to all the kings of the Hittites and the kings of Syria" (I Kings 10:29).

Though some of his domestic policies and his clever trading ventures show a degree of shrewdness, was Solomon really wise? He is credited, to be sure, with authorship of the Book of Proverbs. But even if some of its statements could be ascribed to him, theirs is a wisdom on parchment. In his life, Solomon was not the wisest of men.

He secured for the Hebrews a generation of peace and unparelleled prosperity at a heavy cost that led to smouldering discontent. But was he motivated by service to God and to Israel or by his own self-aggrandizement? He "put Israel on the map" as no one had done before or would do again, but his efforts often seem to be for the sake of his own glory.

A very revealing story is told of him as a young king facing the heavy task of ruling Israel. While sacrificing at the high place in Gibeon, before the temple was built, Solomon dreamed that the Lord appeared and said to him, "Ask what I shall give you" (I Kings 3:5). It is worth noting that to Solomon, God was chiefly the Giver, rather than One Who is to be served, as Moses sought to serve Him all the days of his life. Conscious of his own inadequacy as a young king, Solomon prayed, "Give thy servant therefore an understanding mind to govern thy people, that I may discern between good and evil; for who is able to govern this thy great people?" (I Kings 3:9).

It was a noble petition. Offered anything, Solomon chose nothing material. All he desired, at the moment, was to be a good king.

But then the dream continued. Solomon believed that God would give him not only wisdom but much else besides. "Behold, I give you a wise and discerning mind, so that none like you has been before you and none like you shall arise after you. I give you also what you have not asked, both riches and honor, so that no other king shall compare with you, all your days" (I Kings 3:12-13).

Riches, honor, fame, pre-eminence—these were the gifts Solomon really desired. These were the gifts he received in lavish measure. His glory was greater than that of any of Israel's kings, yet his legacy was an exhausted populace and a divided empire.

Jesus referred to "Solomon in all his glory" as the outstanding example of worldly magnificence; yet He found more wondrous and beautiful the simple God-given adornment of the "lilies of the field" (Matt. 6:28, 29).

XI

J O S I A H

THE REFORMER

ACCESSION OF A BOY KING

Josiah was only eight years old when the people of Judah made him king. The kingdom he was called to lead was not the extensive realm established by David and maintained by Solomon. As we have already noted, the united kingdom was split in two in the beginning of the reign of Solomon's son, Rehoboam. He and his descendants, of whom Josiah was one, ruled the small southern kingdom of Judah from the old capital, Jerusalem.

In the north the ten tribes of Israel, united with Judah-Benjamin by David, but aroused to rebellion by Solomon's policies, finally seceded from his son's kingdom. They became the northern kingdom of Israel, with their capital at Shechem and later at Samaria.

Long before Josiah's time Assyria had risen to dominance in the Euphrates valley and had pushed west and south into the northern kingdom of Israel. With the capture of Israel's capital city of Samaria, in 722 B.C., Assyria completed the conquest of the northern kingdom. Important segments of Israel's population were driven into captivity, in the usual custom of the time, in

125

order to break tribal traditions and cut emotional ties. This insured against later uprisings by the conquered people. So completely did the Assyrians destroy the kingdom of Israel that it never became a thoroughly Hebrew nation again. Its territories were inhabited by a mixed population called the Samaritans, who in New Testament times, as many stories and parables show, were disdained by the Judeans.

But in Judah, Josiah's grandfather Manasseh had saved his kingdom from the political fate of Israel. He made treaties with Assyria that preserved Judah as a nation and gave her nearly a half-century of peace and prosperity. But Judah paid a price for this. Not only was tribute levied by mighty Assyria on the small Hebrew nation, but, more important, Assyria exerted religious pressure. Possibly to placate his overlords, Manasseh adopted many foreign gods, entirely ignoring Yahweh's exclusive claim. His people followed their king's example, so that Hebrew religion was perverted in Judah.

The Scriptures describe Manasseh's apostasy in detail.

For he rebuilt the high places which Hezekiah his father had destroyed; and he erected altars for Baal, and made an Asherah, as Ahab king of Israel had done, and worshiped all the host of heaven, and served them. . . . And he burned his son as an offering, and practiced soothsaying and augury, and dealt with mediums and with wizards.

II Kings 21:3, 6

Horrified that the Lord God of Israel was becoming merely one among the countless heathen gods, the prophets cried out against Manasseh and all his abominations. But they cried in vain, for pagan practices continued throughout his reign. The men of God had to await a more favorable reign before their words would have effect.

Amon followed in his father's footsteps, but not for long.

He seems to have been the victim of a change in the political situation. After its amazing rise to world power, Assyria declined rapidly, strengthening the anti-Assyrian party in Jerusalem. This party may have been responsible for the king's murder.

In times of danger such as this, the democratic element in the nation's political life asserted itself. Now in the year 640 B.C. the people insisted, in opposition to the pro-Assyrian and anti-Assyrian court parties, that Josiah should succeed his murdered father Amon, thus continuing the dynasty of King David.

At first, regents ruled Judah for the boy king, but soon Josiah began to take power into his own hands. At sixteen Josiah first revealed the bent of his mind, for "he began to seek the God of David his father" (II Chron. 34:3). All the faithful must have rejoiced at this sign. Four years later when they saw him begin to "purge Judah and Jerusalem of the high places, the Asherim, and the graven and the molten images," they knew a religious restoration was at hand.

Soon Josiah's drive to cleanse the country of idolatry and the mixed religion of his father and grandfather spread beyond Judah. This would have been impossible if Assyria's grip on her conquered provinces had not slackened. Apparently the Assyrians no longer possessed the military strength to keep the ambitious young king of Judah within his own kingdom.

A significant feature of Josiah's character was its mixture of religious and political motives. When he acted to restore the exclusiveness of Yahweh by designating the temple of Jerusalem as the only place of worship, he ordered the elimination of many sanctuaries throughout the country. This meant that the central power of the king in Jerusalem was considerably strengthened. It also meant that Hebrews still remaining in the former kingdom of Israel were drawn closer to Judah. Josiah must have seen himself as a kind of savior of God's chosen people of Israel.

JEREMIAH'S ESTIMATE OF CONDITIONS

The conditions Josiah tried to correct are recorded in the first six chapters of the Book of Jeremiah. The prophet remembered with longing the beginning of Israel's relation with Yahweh. It had been like a love affair.

> I remember the devotion of your youth,
>   your love as a bride,
> how you followed me in the wilderness,
>   in a land not sown.
> Israel was holy to the Lord.
>
> Jer. 2:2-3

Things were different now.

> Has a nation changed its gods,
>   even though they are no gods?
> But my people have changed their glory
>   for that which does not profit. . . .
> For my people have committed two evils:
>   they have forsaken me,
> the fountain of living waters,
>   and hewed out cisterns for themselves,
> broken cisterns,
>   that can hold no water.
>
> Jer. 2:11, 13

Israel's faith had been completely perverted, for idolatry had found its way into Hebrew religion.

> [You] say to a tree, "You are my father,"
>   and to a stone, "You gave me birth."
>
> Jer. 2:27

The worship of idols made of wood or stone also resulted in great social evils.

Also on your skirts is found
the lifeblood of guiltless poor.
Jer. 2:34

The prophet addressed the king directly. "The Lord said to
me in the days of King Josiah: 'Have you seen what she did,
that faithless one, Israel, how she went up on every high hill and
under every green tree, and there played the harlot?' " (Jer. 3:6).

According to the covenant idea, Judah and Israel should be
one people, as they had been during their years in the desert after
their liberation from Egypt. They should live with their God
like a young married couple, full of love and devotion. The
northern kingdom had already paid for its guilt by falling prey
to the Assyrians. Had the southern kingdom been spared because
it was somehow nobler?

To this question Jeremiah answered, "No." In a startling announcement he declared, "Faithless Israel has shown herself less
guilty than false Judah" (Jer. 3:11). Faced with a difficult
political situation, and without benefit of the sanctuary in Jerusalem, Israel had lost her original faith. Judah, on the other hand,
had become a false people, for, in spite of possessing Yahweh's
sanctuary, they had accepted other gods. They had made Yahweh merely a part of a highly complex mixed religion. Though
worship in the temple still gave the appearance of worship, in-
wardly the faith was destroyed.

Were the steps Josiah had already taken enough? Jeremiah
watched with approval the destruction of images, the defilement
of sanctuaries throughout the land, and the centralization of
worship in Jerusalem. But in the prophet's eyes all this was not
enough. He demanded much more—nothing less than an inner
renewal of men's hearts.

Circumcise yourselves to the Lord,
remove the foreskin of your hearts,
O men of Judah and inhabitants of Jerusalem.
Jer. 4:4

Would a thoroughgoing renewal take place? Jeremiah was not too hopeful that it would. He concluded the sixth chapter of his prophetic book by calling himself an assayer who examined precious metals to determine their qualities. He declared that he had tested Israel and Judah, but had found them to be only base metal.

RESTORATION OF THE TEMPLE

By the eighteenth year of his reign, King Josiah's religious reforms had reached the point when it was time to restore the temple to its original beauty. All traces of special porches and annexes built for other gods were to be removed. In spite of its elaborate ornamentation, Solomon's temple was fundamentally simple, reflecting the exclusiveness of Yahweh.

On the day Josiah decided it was time to begin to repair the temple, he sent his secretary, Shaphan, there to open the collection boxes. These had been placed on the temple grounds to receive the people's offerings for work on the sanctuary. Apparently the money had been accumulating for a long time.

Josiah showed great confidence in the carpenters, masons, architects, and buyers of material, for he ordered that all money should be handed over to them and that no accounting be required of them. He was sure that they would deal honestly with the money of the Lord.

THE BOOK FOUND IN THE TEMPLE

When the king's emissary, Shaphan, reached the temple, he found the high priest Hilkiah waiting for him with a message of importance. Hilkiah must have been looking forward to this opportunity for some time. The priest made his startling announcement, "I have found the book of the law in the house of the Lord" (II Kings 22:8).

What was this volume? It was the book we call Deuteronomy, the fifth in the series of the Five Books of Moses. Deuteronomy means "the second law." In this case it was not an additional law, but the second issue of the same law, with nothing changed except the thought forms in which the ancient truth is expressed.

Where had Hilkiah found this book? Had it been known for a long time, but kept secret until the time was right for its disclosure? We do not know the answers to either of these questions. Nor do we know whether only the core of this book was really ancient. It may or may not have been considerably edited and enlarged to fit the needs of the time.

Shaphan carried the scroll back to the palace to show to the king. At once Josiah was curious about its contents and ordered his secretary to read it to him. The king was so deeply shocked by what he heard that he rent his clothes in sorrow. All the religious reforms he had so far instituted, he saw, were far short of the requirements laid down by this book.

He wondered what the book meant and decided to consult a prophetess named Huldah who lived in Jerusalem. Her reply was that the judgment of Yahweh would certainly come, but that Josiah himself would not see the evil that would befall Judah, because he had been penitent and had tried to recover the original faith for his people.

DESTRUCTION AND REBUILDING

Feverish activity filled the next years of Josiah's reign. It was characteristic of the man to do things completely, to destroy faster than he could rebuild. Everything that had altered the religious image of the Hebrews and had denied the exclusiveness of Yahweh was to be uprooted. Idolatry, mixed religious activities, even the many places of genuine Hebrew worship outside Jerusalem were to be swept away.

There are grave consequences when everything that does not completely conform to the ideal is removed. Such destruction creates a vacuum which is often not filled with truth, but with new idolatries, new cynicism, or, what is worse, mere external compliance with the new forms.

Josiah was convinced that he was only recovering what had been lost. He wanted to get back to the simple, original form which had been overlaid by the debris of centuries. So far no reformation has achieved such a goal, because the clock cannot be reversed. One cannot return to the good old days when everything seemed right and true. Man sees the past with the eyes of the present. Thus religious restoration becomes a progression into something new, rooted in the old, but in itself a new creation, a drive toward a cleaner, better faith.

The problem of any reformation is, what should be swept away, what should be conserved. The wise reformer retains as much as possible of the old in order to keep the confidence of his own generation. To impress the new direction on the masses, he destroys only significant symbols. He deals with essentials, leaving less important changes to develop naturally.

Though the harshness of Josiah's policies may have been justified, his reform failed because it ignored human nature. His reformation lacked concern for the common man, for his inability to understand new principles and to apply these readily to all his actions. When the Book of Deuteronomy and the prophet Jeremiah speak of a circumcision of the heart, they refer to an inner rather than a radical external change. Josiah, too, wanted an inner change, but he did not know how to achieve it.

In defense of Josiah, it must be said that the religious situation in Jerusalem and throughout the whole land, as described in II Kings 23:4-14, must have been horrible to those who tried to remain faithful. One has the impression that there was more true Yahweh worship in the small Hebrew settlements outside of Palestine than in Judah and Israel themselves.

The temptation to be radical must have seemed strong to a young man of twenty-five. It was with the conviction that he was absolutely right, while his adversaries were absolutely wrong, that Josiah enthusiastically destroyed images and smashed idols, defiling them with all the means at his disposal. In his zeal for the pure faith, theology and correct ritual became more important than love for his fellow man. As the individual today is frequently disregarded in favor of the "organization," so Josiah sacrificed the rights of people for his idea of reform.

Step by step, as the king's efforts to purify religion extended throughout Judah and into the former territory of Israel, so his political control also advanced.

EGYPT THE ENEMY

By this time Assyria had become a weak and fragmented empire posing no threat to Egypt. Pharaoh Neco of the twenty-sixth dynasty began his reign by marching against Judean forces along the old coastal road which turned east at Mount Carmel into the Plain of Jezreel, from which it ran north to Damascus and beyond.

Josiah confronted Neco in a decisive battle overlooking the Plain of Jezreel, near the strategic location of Megiddo, where long ago the Israelites under Deborah and Barak had defeated Sisera. If the king had been able to withstand the Egyptians here, deep within the vanquished kingdom of Israel, he would have restored David's kingdom. This would have crowned all his efforts and won fame for him as restorer of the house of David and savior of Yahweh's people.

All this was not to be. Huldah's prophecy concerning the end of Judah was about to come true. In the Hebrew understanding of history, Pharaoh Neco was an instrument of God's holy will. Therefore, he could rightly say to Josiah, "Cease opposing God, who is with me" (II Chron. 35:21).

The king was unable to understand this contradiction. Surely the Lord was on Judah's side, not Egypt's. Would not a successful stand against Neco at Megiddo give back to the Lord territory that was His?

In this belief Josiah "joined battle in the plain of Megiddo. And the archers shot King Josiah; and the king said to his servants, 'Take me away, for I am badly wounded' " (II Chron. 35:22-23).

From the battlefield he was carried by chariot back to Jerusalem where he died and was buried in the tomb of his fathers.

ESTIMATE OF JOSIAH

Throughout his reign Josiah acted from the best of intentions, deeply convinced that he was doing the Lord's will. He considered himself chosen by God to restore the united kingdom, not for his own gain, but to rebuild the covenant people, *as he understood* it. But the way he went about it—his insistence on speedy change, his inability to understand his people's feelings, his natural fusion of secular and spiritual gain—all helped to dig the grave of his nation.

He did, however, leave them a valuable legacy in the Book of Deuteronomy. In his reign the covenant was renewed and a Passover celebrated, the first in a long time. These were seeds for a new future, to be born, after great pain and travail, through an inner reconstruction.

XII

E Z R A

THE TEACHER

BABYLONIAN CAPTIVITY

Ezra, the man who became the founder of Judaism, emerged as a leader some time after the Babylonian captivity. He added a new dimension to the Hebrew religion without changing its basic tenets. As a result of his labors, Hebrew faith lived on in Judaism and continued as a basic element in Christianity. To understand this man and the unusual contribution he made to his people, we must consider their situation at the end of their seventy years of captivity.

During the reign of Zedekiah, Josiah's son and the last Davidic king, the Babylonian conquerors captured Jerusalem in 587 B.C. and deported many of the inhabitants of Judah into captivity in far-off Babylon.

Less than a century and a half earlier this same disaster had overtaken the northern kingdom of Israel. In that case the people had not been permitted to live together, to continue their religious activities, or to maintain any kind of national or ethnic identity. Only people of the lower social stratum had been allowed to remain in the land of the Ten Tribes, which was then repopulated with newcomers. The ensuing mixture of peoples meant the end of a Hebrew nation in the North.

The Babylonians treated their Judean captives quite differently, permitting them to live in close touch with each other. The new area to which they were exiled apparently offered employment to skills that had not been utilized in their Judean homeland. When they became traders and artisans, their educational and cultural level rose.

Babylonian religious expressions were so colorful and so full of pageantry that they failed to attract the exiles. As they were permitted to have their own priests and their own worship, they began to develop strong religious convictions in contrast to their environment.

PROPHETS OF THE EXILE

During the seventy years while the Judeans lived in Babylonia, the spirit of prophecy flourished among them. Vigorous prophetic voices infused new strength into Hebrew religious life. The so-called Second Isaiah, whose writings begin in Chapter 40 in the Isaiah scroll, belongs to this time, as do also the later words of Jeremiah.

The strongest personality among these prophets was that of Ezekiel. In Chapter 34 of his book he creates an impressive vision which brought assurance to the Hebrews that Yahweh planned a great revival for them. This chapter describing the valley of dry bones has stirred the imaginations of many writers and artists and formed the basis for one of America's great spirituals. Ezekiel wrote,

The hand of the Lord was upon me, and he brought me out by the Spirit of the Lord, and set me down in the midst of the valley; it was full of bones. . . . and lo, they were very dry. And he said to me, "Son of man, can these bones live?" And I answered, "O Lord God, thou knowest." Again he said to me, "Prophesy to these bones, and say to them, O dry bones, hear the word of the Lord. . . ."

So I prophesied as I was commanded; and as I prophesied, there was a noise, and behold, a rattling; and the bones came together, bone to its bone.   Ezek. 37:1-7

Ezekiel saw the bones rejoin and become covered with sinews, flesh, and skin, but still they were only shells of life.

Then he said to me, "Prophesy to the breath, prophesy, son of man, and say to the breath, Thus says the Lord God: Come from the four winds, O breath, and breathe upon these slain, that they may live. . . ."

Then he said to me, "Son of man, these bones are the whole house of Israel. Behold, they say, 'Our bones are dried up, and our hope is lost. . . .' Thus says the Lord God: Behold, I will open your graves, and raise you from your graves, O my people; and I will bring you home into the land of Israel."   Ezek. 37:9-12

OTHER RELIGIOUS DEVELOPMENTS

In Babylonia the Hebrews had no temple and were thus forced to find another form of public religious expression and religious community. The synagogue grew out of these needs. It had no altar upon which sacrifices could be offered, nor was the chief activity of the synagogue that of worship. Its primary function was to bring the people together in the never-ending search for knowledge of the Law.

In the Babylonian period of its origin, the synagogue did not meet all the religious needs. It did not reach everyone, nor did it create a fully trained religious community, but it made possible the survival of Judaism to this day.

Another product of the exile and possibly of the endless religious discussions in the synagogues was the Book of Job, which many scholars believe was written during this time. Job personifies the sufferings experienced by the entire body of Judeans.

The book raises the problem of the justice of God and its kindred question—why must good men suffer? To exiles waiting for the fulfillment of Jeremiah's prophecy that they would return to their own land after seventy years of captivity, Job brought comfort in his great answer affirming the impressive majesty of the Creator of heaven and earth.

CYRUS AND POLITICAL CHANGE

In 588 B.C. when Cyrus ascended the throne of Anshan, a small desert kingdom on the edge of Babylonian territories, few could have guessed the enormous changes this ambitious military genius would bring about. By 550 B.C. he was master of Ecbatana, the capital city of the Medes. Four years later he moved against the Lydians in Asia Minor, defeating King Croesus, renowned for his fabulous wealth, and occupying his capital of Sardis. Seven years after that conquest, Cyrus took the Chaldean empire and was ready to attack the city of Babylon.

He stationed his troops around the well-fortified city, which had been supplied with provisions for a twenty-year siege. Inside the city, Belshazzar ruled—the king served by Daniel the Judean.

During a rousing feast the king saw a hand writing unknown letters on the wall. When he asked the learned Daniel to interpret the strange writing, he was given its meaning: "MENE, God has numbered the days of your kingdom and brought it to an end; TEKEL, you have been weighed in the balances and found wanting; PERES, your kingdom is divided and given to the Medes and Persians" (Dan. 5:26-28).

That same night Cyrus made a surprise attack on Babylon. He had ordered his men to dig drainage ditches around the city. When these were opened the waters of the Euphrates River flowed into them leaving the river bed dry. Cyrus' troops used this as a road into the heart of the city. Traces of this diversion of the river are still visible in the ruins of Babylon. Thus in 539 b.c., Cyrus overwhelmed the Babylonian empire and occupied its capital almost without a struggle.

Cyrus proved to be a progressive leader with a new and surprising policy toward subject nations. He did not follow the usual custom of such conquerors as the Assyrians and Babylonians, who drove conquered enemies from their homeland into captivity and tried to force different gods upon them. King Cyrus dreamed of a closely-knit commonwealth made up of individual states free to develop their own way of life. Throughout his dominions Cyrus was represented by governors called satraps who were instructed not to interfere with the people of their provinces unless the safety of the empire was threatened.

Cyrus reigned from the deserts of Lybia in North Africa to the borders of what is now southern Russia, from the Indus River in India to Macedonia in Greece, and from the Arabian Desert to the Caucasus Mountains. This great conqueror dreamed of world-wide domination and an era of peace.

Immediately after the fall of Babylon, Cyrus decreed that all captives then living in exile should be released and permitted to return to their homelands. Moreover, he offered them aid for their return journey.

Second Isaiah, in true Hebrew fashion, saw history as God's work and Cyrus as God's anointed one, acting from divine inspiration.

> Thus says the Lord to his anointed, to Cyrus,
> whose right hand I have grasped,
> to subdue nations before him. . . .
> "I will go before you

and level the mountains . . .
that you may know that it is I, the Lord,
the God of Israel, who call you by your name. . . ."

Isa. 45:1-3

RETURN FROM EXILE

The first group of Hebrew exiles returned to their own land under Sheshbazzar, one of the princes of Judah whom Cyrus appointed governor of Judah. With him went Zerubbabel, a prince of the house of David, and Jeshua, a grandson of probably the last high priest in Jerusalem before its destruction. The group of exiles travelled on foot along the caravan routes linking Babylon and Jerusalem, a distance of a little less than a thousand miles. The beasts of burden mentioned in the Bible must have been needed to carry the temple treasures which had been looted by the Babylonians but were now being returned by Cyrus.

For the Hebrews the return from exile was another Exodus, another return from captivity to the Promised Land. As in the first Exodus, they journeyed through the desert, and there were many among the weary travellers who wished they had not left the comfortable security of captivity.

In October, 538 B.C., the returned exiles erected the first simple altar on Mount Zion, again on the threshing floor of Araunah, where David had built his first altar after capturing the city from the Jebusites. According to tradition, Abraham had prepared to sacrifice Isaac on this holy rock. Here stood the Holy of Holies of Solomon's temple, or the altar before it. Centuries later on the same spot, the Muslims built the Dome of the Rock, the mosque of Omar which stands there today. The Koran says that from this rock the prophet Mohammed was lifted by angels. The Jews who returned labored to restore Israel's religion in this sacred place so rich in Hebrew tradition.

EZRA'S WORK

Ezra's reconstruction was not so much one of masonry as of an inner restoration. He transformed the Hebrew religion from its original state, centered in the tent of meeting, the Ark of the Covenant, and the sacrifice on the altar of Yahweh, to a religion of the Book. To be sure, the temple was rebuilt, and for centuries to come sacrifices were offered there. Until its destruction in 70 A.D., it remained, with certain interruptions, the ritual center of Israel. But the religious life of Judaism, in the homeland as well as in the far-flung diaspora, was in the reading and study of Israel's Law, the Torah. This change of emphasis, which resulted in the Jews becoming the so-called "People of the Book," was partly a result of Ezra's efforts.

Ezra's work of enshrining a book at the heart of Hebrew religion lies behind not only the emphasis of Jews upon the Word of God but the Christian belief that Jesus Christ is His living Word.

EZRA AS SCHOOLMASTER

A graphic story of how Ezra taught the law to the people is told in the eighth chapter of the book of Nehemiah.

Early in the morning on a given date, there gathered in the square before the Water Gate a full assembly of "men and women and all who could hear with understanding" the Law of Moses about which Ezra had talked to them. (Neh. 8:2).

Ezra stood high above the crowd in a wooden pulpit which had been especially made for him. There he "opened the book in the sight of all the people, for he was above all the people; and when he opened it all the people stood" (Neh. 8:5).

After an appropriate blessing, Ezra began to read. But this was not to be a simple reading of the Scriptures. On Ezra's right and left stood groups of Levites whose names are carefully recorded. These men were prepared to give instruction. The people were first divided into classes and then, after Ezra had read portions of the Law, the Levites "helped the people to understand the law, while the people remained in their places . . . they gave the sense, so that the people understood the reading" (Neh. 8:7-8).

Here for the first time in the Scriptures, the duty of the Levites is mentioned. The Levite was the prototype of the rabbi whose task it is to read correctly and to interpret what he reads, in order to promote understanding. The priest's duty was service at the altar. In the parable of the Good Samaritan, a distinction is made between priests and Levites.

Ezra realized that the Word of God as recorded in the Scriptures, for him specifically the Law of Moses, is not a closed book, but a book of basic truth that always needs adaptation.

"THE JOY OF THE LORD IS YOUR STRENGTH"

As the first reading of the Law progressed, sounds of sorrow swept over the assembly. "For all the people wept when they heard of the words of the law" (Neh. 8:9).

We can imagine how they must have felt. When they had gathered in the square that morning, they thought they were good Jews. Had they not given up excellent positions in Babylon and crossed the weary miles of desert to rebuild the Holy Land? In response to the call of their inspired prophets, and for the sake of their own convictions, they had borne much hardship. But what did they really know about their ancient faith? The reading showed them that they knew very little indeed. The realization of the poverty of their religion broke their hearts. An inner restoration of faith was needed.

Though Ezra was primarily a schoolmaster whose greatest achievement was that of developing a Bible-trained congregation, his second achievement was equal to the first, for he gave his people joy in their faith, joy in their religion, joy in truth. When sounds of mourning swept the assembly, Ezra's voice rang out to lift his people up again.

This day is holy to the Lord your God; do not mourn or weep. . . . Go your way, eat the fat and drink sweet wine and send portions to him for whom nothing is prepared; for this day is holy to our Lord; and do not be grieved, for the joy of the Lord is your strength.   Neh. 8:9-10

RENEWING THE COVENANT

The book-centered religion developed by Ezra was ideally suited to the foundation laid down in the Law, the historical books, and the writings of the prophets. Like these records of Israel's religious insight, Ezra perceived the sweep of human events as holy history. His God was the God of Abraham and of Isaac and of Jacob, the God who led Israel out of Egypt, the God who led them into Babylonian captivity, and the God who at this moment had restored them to their own land. This is the living God who reveals Himself in continuous historical action with His people.

In view of his beliefs, it was natural that under Ezra the covenant was renewed. Nehemiah 10 records the names of those who set their seal upon the new document of the covenant.

EZRA'S LEGALISM

It is perhaps to be expected that a person as fanatically devoted to the Law as Ezra was, should have shortcomings. His single-track mind and his severe legalistic outlook were responsible for one of the largest mass divorces in history.

The matter of intermarriages with other peoples was brought to Ezra's attention by officials in Jerusalem, probably unnecessarily, because it is unlikely that he was not aware of the situation. Even members of priestly families had taken foreign wives, so that, in the words of the report, "the holy race has mixed itself with the peoples of the lands. And in this faithlessness the hand of the officials and chief men has been foremost" (Ezra 9:2).

The problem concerned only the foreign wives of Hebrew men. As far back as Ezra the regulation applied that the mother determines the religious future of her child. The rule was that you were a Jew if born of Jewish mother whether or not your father was a Jew.

When he consulted the Law of Moses, Ezra found that it did not permit intermarriage with enemies of Israel who had resisted their entry into the Promised Land. This law provided a basis for his action. Ezra revised the statute by bringing it up to date. He declared, "Therefore let us make a covenant with our God to put away all these wives and their children" (Ezra 10:3).

The names of those who had married foreign wives are duly recorded and at the end of the list appears the fateful sentence: "All these had married foreign women, and they put them away with their children" (Ezra 10:44).

This mass self-cleansing of Israel was not a matter of racial discrimination as we understand that term today. The term "race," as we define it, is an invention of the nineteenth and twentieth centuries. Foreign wives in Israel raised a religious, not a racial problem. Ezra wanted to keep Israel religiously pure, undefiled by idolatrous religions which foreign mothers would inevitably introduce into Jewish homes. There is no mention made of divorcing foreign fathers. Though they would cause as much mingling of "races," in the modern sense, as would the foreign mothers, children of such foreign fathers would not be brought up in alien faiths.

In spite of the cruelty and heartache produced by Ezra's vision of a religiously pure Israel and by his legalism in carrying out his ideas, Ezra accomplished much for his people. He insisted on correct ritual, especially in reviving the important festivals, but his chief interest was in the clear understanding of God's will by continued learning of the Law.

From the days of Moses and the giving of the Law at Mount Sinai, the Hebrews had come full circle. They had grown and developed as a nation under the kings, but had lived through a decline of religious purity during the years following the division of the kingdom. In Babylonia they had suffered another captivity only to survive for another Exodus through the desert. Again they had reached Jerusalem, where Ezra and Nehemiah and other leaders re-established their religion on the durable foundation of the Law and the covenant.

What their faith still lacked was the element of love which, in the New Testament, is seen as the true fulfillment of the Law. The consolidation of Jewish religious ideas in the period after the return from exile leaves open the door for Christ, the Messiah, to enter.

Suggestions for Further Reading

The most important text for continued study is, of course, the Bible itself. The serious student should read the Scriptures in more than one version. The variations among different translations help to free us from bondage to mere words and to keep us open to new insights and meaning.

Two useful aids to Bible study are a concordance and an atlas. The concordance enables the reader to locate any passage quickly and promotes understanding of the text by permitting comparison of word usage in different verses. A Bible atlas provides a graphic picture of the geographical setting for events recorded in the Scriptures. A number of good concordances and atlases are available.

Many books provide a treatment of the text and background of the Old Testament which will be useful to the general reader. The following list is limited to a few titles that may be helpful for particular purposes. The extensive bibliographies in these volumes, especially those by Anderson and Sandmel, should be consulted by those who wish to pursue intensive study of special aspects of the Bible.

Westermann, Claus. *A Thousand Years and a Day: Our Time in the Old Testament.* Philadelphia: Fortress Press, 1962. One of the best books covering the entire Old Testament for the non-academic reader.

Napier, B. Davie. *Song of the Vineyard.* New York: Harper & Row, 1962. A theological introduction.

Anderson, Bernhard W. *Understanding the Old Testament.* Englewood Cliffs: Prentice-Hall, 1957. A textbook that can be read by the layman.

McKenzie, John L. *The Two-Edged Sword.* Milwaukee: Bruce Publishing Co., 1956. An interpretation of the Old Testament from the Roman Catholic viewpoint.

Sandmel, Samuel. *The Hebrew Scriptures.* New York: Alfred A. Knopf, Inc., 1963. An exposition of the Hebrew Bible from the Jewish standpoint.

Anderson, Bernhard W., ed. *The Old Testament and Christian Faith.* New York: Harper & Row, 1963. A stimulating discussion of an important problem, on a more advanced level.